FUNNY LONDON
THE CAPITAL'S HUMOUR HERITAGE

TOM KING

AMBERLEY

To Evie, Josh and Felix

Other Books by the Author
The Southend Story (with Kevan Furbank)
King & Country
Thames Estuary Trail
Footpaths: A British History

First published 2026

Amberley Publishing
The Hill, Stroud,
Gloucestershire, GL5 4EP

www.amberley-books.com

ISBN: 978 1 3981 2828 6 (print)
ISBN: 978 1 3981 2829 3 (ebook)

British Library Cataloguing in Publication Data.
A catalogue record for this book is available from the British Library.

Typeset in 10pt on 13pt Celeste.
Origination by Amberley Publishing.
Printed in the UK.

Appointed GPSR EU Representative:
Easy Access System Europe Oü, 16879218
Address: Mustamäe tee 50, 10621, Tallinn, Estonia
Contact Details: gpsr.requests@easproject.com, +358 40 500 3575

Contents

1

Introduction

The wider world has tended to approach London – ancient royal city, home to the mother of parliaments, Churchillian citadel of war – with a certain sense of gravity. Unlike the city itself and its inhabitants. They have never taken themselves too seriously.

Laughter has always flourished as a key part of the city's identity. It is the birthright of every Londoner. The composer Sir Edward Elgar, for one, rated it high among the

The very emblem of London and its humour: Mr Punch. The rowdy little puppet Punch was born in a Covent Garden booth around 1660. But in London, he subsequently evolved into a genial, avuncular figure, partly modelled on Dickens's Samuel Pickwick, and acquired the more respectable 'Mr' title along the way. As the nominal editor-in-chief of *Punch* magazine, he presided over the most widely read humorous journal ever published. *Punch*'s team of writers and artists trawled the streets of London in search of comic material that kept the world laughing on a weekly basis (see pp. 48–49, 55, 72, 78).

components of the city's natives. Writing his *Cockaigne* overture, he sought to capture the humour in music, with notes that were 'cheerful and Londony, stout and steaky ... honest, healthy, humorous and strong'.

The strength, good health and humour noted by Elgar are not separate qualities, but closely interconnected ones. Londoners really have tended to the conviction that humour is health, and laughter, indeed, the best of medicines. In 1665, as the plague descended on London, wealthier citizens fled the capital for the safety of the countryside. But Samuel Pepys, the diarist and naval administrator, was one of those who chose to remain. Whole families of neighbours in Pepys's street, Seething Lane, were wiped out by the plague, but Sam remained hale and hearty throughout. He attributed his survival to constant merrymaking. He and a group of friends gathered to tell one another funny stories that 'did make us all die almost with laughing'.

Can any other city have developed its humour along so many different lines, from the raucous antics of the miracle plays to the daily newspaper cartoons and comedy revues that kept London laughing through the Blitz? At all times, London street life has had a tendency to erupt into unscripted and often bizarre comic scenes. The city's social history sometimes takes on the air of a non-stop run of Monty Python.

Londoners have laughed at everything under the sun and beyond it. Most particularly, though, they have always laughed at London itself. This is indeed a city that has never quite mastered the art of taking itself too seriously, because the old place is just intrinsically funny. London's humour is unshakeable, because it rests on a deep sub-stratum, formed from an age-old and pulsating glee in life's vagaries and absurdities.

The Thames flows on eternally, and so does the supply of books dealing with London's history. Yet strangely, London's humour, such a core aspect of its past, has been overlooked. *Funny London* aims to make a start, at least, in redressing that omission. Laughter is indeed the best medicine, and Londoners should remember the prescription. *Funny London* comes off the press during a worrisome time for the world. But humour – and an awareness of the benign power of humour – has helped the city through even grimmer times in the past, and its old healing medicine could prove invaluable again, in years to come ...

The statue of Celtic warrior queen Boudica at Westminster Pier, poised to trample all over the modern tourist trade just as she rampaged over Roman London in AD 61. It remains an enduring mystery why London should have erected a statue to a woman who annihilated it, but down the years, 'Boudicea [*sic*] and Her Daughters' has proved a magnet for jokesters. Rampant misogynists dubbed it: 'Depiction of the first woman MP entering Parliament.' In the days of hand signals (and still rampant chauvinism), tourist guides used to pose the question: 'Why did Boudica fail her driving test?' to which the answer was: 'Because she has her arm pointed left, while turning right.'

2

Roman Humour Then and Now

The Romans liked to laugh. Emperors doubled as jokesters, and laughter was included among the pleasures of imperial life. Claudius – in whose reign the full conquest of Britannia began – was renowned for his witty remarks. Comedy and humour (both Graeco-Latin words in their origin) were exported to all cities of the western empire, along with the wine, the baths and the underfloor heating. Among the recipients would have been London, which by the second century had grown to be the largest city north of the Alps.

However, Roman Londinium's laughter has left no echoes. No old jokes have been excavated from London soil, and none of the skeletal remains suggest that anyone died laughing. But it seems inconceivable that Roman Brits would have failed to import humour as an accepted aspect of the good life.

We know that ancient Romans enjoyed a joke, not least because the reign of Emperor Gratian (367–83) saw the publication of the world's oldest-surviving joke book, the *Philogelos*. The *Philogelos* was widely read and its contents widely quoted across the Roman Empire.

The *Philogelos*, compiled by two Greeks, Hierocles and Philagrios, is the ultimate proof of the fact that there is no such thing as a new joke. Gags that were knocking around the Roman Empire were still being told in London pubs and street markets two millennia later. In the East End, in particular, everyone seems to have read and spread the jokes in the *Philogelos*. The rabbi and broadcaster Lionel Blue, who grew up in the Mile End Road, made a point of logging these jokes and their ancient ancestry.

One anecdote in particular serves to underline the continuity of London humour from the age of the Roman emperors to the reign of King Charles III.

The resident hairdresser in the Houses of Parliament was, for many years, a notoriously garrulous individual. He would prattle non-stop as he snipped. MPs, shackled to the barber's chair, sat powerless, unable, for once, to get a word in edgeways.

Then came the day when Enoch Powell MP came to sit in the chair. Powell was abhorred by many for his politics, but admired universally as a classical scholar, and as possibly the wittiest person in Parliament.

The hairdresser asked the usual question, 'How should I cut your hair, sir?'

Powell's riposte was instantaneous. 'In silence.'

This remark was immediately bandied around Westminster and beyond as another instance of Powell's sharp wit.

The man himself never denied ownership of the remark, but in fact he had borrowed it from his beloved ancient Rome. The authors of the *Philogelos* considered it so hilarious that they printed the exchange several times over in the pages of their book. In their case, the haircutter is a slave rather than a fancy self-employed London stylist, but in other respects, the joke is, word for word, identical.

The ancient Romans' sense of humour is also apparent in their devotion to stage comedy, which amounted to a sizable industry across four centuries. Roman comedy turned up one writer of genius, in the shape of Plautus. He was so good, and so popular, that fake plays 'by Plautus' continued to appear decades after the man himself had died, and one young playwright paid Plautus the ultimate accolade.

That devotee was William Shakespeare. Around 1592, the Bard made what may have been his first stab at a comedy, taking care that it was identified as such in its title. The plot and characters were lifted directly from Plautus's *Menaechmi.*

The Comedy of Errors had its earliest recorded performance at Grays Inn Hall in 1594. Thus did Roman comedy, dormant but not dead for over a millennium, re-emerge, proving once again that you can bury a source of mirth, but you can't kill it.

The peaceful precincts of Grays Inn, with Grays Inn Hall in the background. *The Comedy of Errors* was staged here as a highlight of the 1594 Christmas revels, the first recorded performance of Shakespeare's early comedy. Its plot and characters were shamelessly lifted from the Roman play *Menaechmi* by Plautus.

A direct link exits between the ancient Roman comedy dramatist Plautus and an elegant terrace in one of Kensington's most sought-after residential locations, Edwarde's Square. The house with the blue plate was the home of the comedian Frankie Howerd OBE. Howerd's career was in the doldrums until given a double boost, courtesy of two roles created by Plautus: Pseudolus, the lead figure in the stage musical *A Funny Thing Happened on the Way to the Forum*, and resourceful slave Lurcio in the BBC sitcom *Up Pompeii!* The proceeds allowed Howerd to acquire his high-end Kensington property. Perhaps in gratitude, Plautus himself, played by Willie Rushton, was given regular pop-up appearances in *Up Pompeii!*

Buried Roman comedy certainly was, however. The collapse of Roman power in the early fifth century had a severe effect on London, indeed a virtually terminal one. After 457, when there is a last plaintive record about the survivors of a battle, the place just vanishes – a feat which would be rather harder to achieve nowadays.

Yet aspects of Roman culture somehow lingered on among the ruins. One of these was the annual festival known as the Saturnalia. Everyone loved the Saturnalia. The poet Catullus called it 'the best of times'. There was feasting and dancing, and the wine flowed freely. Masked actors worked their way through the crowds, enacting dramas on the hoof. An unusual feature of these performances highlighted the overall mood of the Saturnalia. Only comedy masks were worn. Tragic or grim face coverings had no place there.

In the early years after the Norman Conquest, the Saturnalia re-erupted as a feature of London life. It now bore a Christian gloss and a new name, the Feast of Fools. But it was still essentially the same old, wild, festival. In 1279, a colourful scandal testified to its resurgence and the extent to which it had permeated the medieval city. Comedy was back in town.

The Cornhill Devils, presiding over the entrance to St Peter-upon-Cornhill, provide a jocular link between Roman and medieval London. The ancient church, now largely hidden from street view, stands on the site of the Great Basilica, the focal structure of law and government in Roman London. There is convincing evidence that St Peter was London's first Christian church, established 500 years before St Paul's. St Peter occupies the highest point in the City of London. The very slender shop fronting Cornhill was built in 1893 by architect Ernest Augustus Runtz. It accidentally encroached onto approximately 1 inch of St Peter's space, much to the fury of the rector and possibly St Peter himself as well. The entire building project had to start again from scratch. But the architect took his revenge in the shape of the devils, medievally-inspired statues of demons. The face of the pictured devil is said to be that of the rector who caused all the trouble.

3

Of Fools and Farce: Medieval London

In 1279, the Archbishop of Canterbury, John Peckham, wrote a stinking letter to the abbess of Barking Abbey foundation, the largest convent in Northern Europe. In choice Latin terms, he admonished her for the way that the abbey's Christmastide miracle play had turned rogue. Comic exuberance had infiltrated what was supposed to be a deeply solemn event. The cast was meant to consist entirely of nuns, and the production was supposed to take place within the abbey walls. Instead, the performers had been local townspeople, the play had been held in the streets of Barking, and it had been the occasion of *insalubris ludicra* (unwholesome frolics), and *comoediae stultum* (foolish comedy). A century before *The Canterbury Tales*, this may represent the first written mention of comedy in the London area. It was far from the last.

In many respects, medieval London was Merry England personified. Despite the fact that life could be brutish and short, or rather, perhaps, because of this fact, its pleasures were relished with true intensity.

The ruins of Barking Abbey, once the largest convent north of the Alps. In 1279, its Christmas miracle play spilled out into the streets of Barking, resulting in 'unwholesome frolics and mirth', seemingly instigated by the nuns themselves.

The hustle and bustle of merry medieval London as depicted by the artist Macdonald Gill. Note the grins on all the faces. (*Rhymes of Old London Town 1916*)

A simple working day could be a revel from dawn to dusk. London streets were essentially one big marketplace. They were places of amusement-seeking as well as commerce, in so far as the two could be separated. The medievalist G. G. Coulton describes London street life as an ongoing 'comedy' that frequently turned into 'a Rabelaisian farce'.

For a glimpse of the comedy, we can turn to the early-fifteenth-century poem 'London Lickpenny'. While exploring London marketplaces, the poet finds that his hood has suddenly gone missing. In search of new headgear, he follows the cry 'New caps!' to a stall in Cornhill. There he finds his own hood, up for sale and marked as new.

This switch from mere comedy to wild farce happened at regular intervals, thanks to the hue and cry. The shout would go up 'Stop thief!'. The crowd instantaneously transformed itself into an ad hoc posse. Stalls were overturned, honest citizens landed headfirst in horse troughs and horses panicked. Sometimes a desperate fugitive resorted to a manoeuvre that, one day, would become a staple of cartoon comedy. The thinness of house walls, often no more than mud, twigs and lathe, meant that a fugitive could crash straight through one wall, run through the house and crash back out through the opposite wall. But he left behind him a vaguely man-shaped cavity and a clear giveaway as to his route.

Watching this vibrant street life from his lodgings, high up in the Aldgate tower, was the government administrator and part-time scribbler Geoffrey Chaucer. Eventually, he put his observations to good narrative-poetic use in a work that captures the teeming energy of medieval London.

The Canterbury Tales plonks us straight into a London tavern on the south side of London Bridge, the Tabard. A diverse assembly, representing a complete cross-section of English society, is preparing to go on a pilgrimage to the tomb of St Thomas à Becket in Canterbury.

The bossy Host of the tavern then suggests, or rather imposes, a scheme that will keep them all amused during the journey. Each pilgrim will tell four different tales, two on the way to Canterbury, two on the return journey.

The enclosed precinct of Ely Place, Holborn, acted as a place of security for pickpockets and other felons operating in Cornhill-Cheapside Market. Any hue and cry in pursuit of them had to stop short at the gates. The ground was owned by the Bishops of Ely and therefore outside the jurisdiction of the London authorities.

The Canterbury Pilgrims, as envisioned by artist Adam Kossowski in a 20,000-piece mosaic mural, inspired by Geoffrey Chaucer's great and comical poetic work *The Canterbury Tales*. The artwork stands alongside the Old Kent Road, the highway taken by the pilgrims on their way from London Bridge to Canterbury.

A fountain now marks the site in Aldgate of the 'Old Gate' that gave the area its name. The fortified gatehouse straddled the main Roman road east to Chelmsford, Colchester and Norwich. Geoffrey Chaucer lived in rooms within the Old Gate tower. The eyrie provided a grandstand view of the teeming life below – rich material for Chaucer's comic tales.

The tales range across every subject and mood, but the largest single category is the comical. Humorous or light-hearted tales account for more than a third of the total. This is partly, at least, under instruction from the Host, who sets the agenda for fun. Roaring Londoner that he is, Mein Host is determined that laughter will ripple from one end of the horseback procession to the other, and back again, all the way from London to Canterbury.

A merrie man ... he spake of mirth ...
And said thus: ...
'Fain would I doon [donate] you mirth
And of a mirth I am right now bethought.'

Chaucer had one great advantage over most other Londoners. He was literate. He had ink and paper, and he had readers. But the great majority of the city population could neither write nor read. Instead, they found another way to turn the foibles and antics of their fellow Londoners into entertainment.

A mumming event at the Tower of London, *c.* 1470, gets somewhat out of hand. (Cartoon by George Cruikshank)

Mumming plays were a strange and anarchic subtext to society. Mumming was at its most active around Christmas but also had a habit of popping up suddenly on a London street, any time, any place. The core of a mumming play was always the same. Two characters would fight, one would be killed and then the third central character, the Doctor, would administer aid and revive the corpse. A comic horse also figured, who was not so much the ancestor of the modern pantomime horse/cow as the enduring template. This original cast was steadily bolstered by a range of other personalities, ranging from fat Friar Tuck to Simple Simon, the archetype of the naive country boy adrift in the big city.

Humour, then, was a quickfire forcefield that darted through the streets of medieval London, lightening and smoothing out the hardships of life. Yet while laughter might have been a tool of many trades, the notion of humour *as* a trade, of earning one's living by laughter alone, was still inconceivable. Humour remained a strictly amateur affair.

Behind the walls of the royal palaces at Westminster and the Tower of London, it was a different story. One person at court earned his livelihood by making mirth. He was, of course, the court jester, paid, housed and fed with the sole purpose of keeping king and court amused.

Jesters were masters of all the comedic techniques that still keep audiences laughing. Take pratfalls, for instance. Morris Ken, jester to the short-lived Edward II, specialised in horseplay, literally. At Windsor, it is recorded, 'he rode ... before the king and often fell from his horse, at which the king laughed exceeding'.

Most jesters were lowly and anonymous. Once the laughter faded away, so did the joker. Yet court jesting was not necessarily a dead-end job, as proven by the spectacular career of the London jester Rahere. We first hear of Rahere at the court of Henry I (king from 1100 to 1135), where he made himself popular with 'coshyns, japes and flatterynges' (verbal and practical jests and flattery). From there, he moved onwards and upwards. He became the organiser of elaborate comic 'spectaclis', which included 'merys, playes and other courtly mokkys and trifyllys'.

Somehow, at some stage, the resourceful Rahere managed to sidestep from the roles of jester and comic impresario into the Church. By the time of his second appearance in the chronicles, he has set aside his jester's cap and bells and is now a high-ranking priest. He accumulated a great deal of wealth, as churchmen often did in those days. He used the money to found the Church of St Bartholomew the Great, and its linked hospital, which grew to become one of London's great centres of medical training and learning. All this by making men laugh.

The elaborate tomb of Rahere, court jester turned leading churchman, takes pride of place inside the church that he founded, St Bartholomew the Great.

Rahere's own tomb occupies a place of honour within St Bart's. It is topped by a full-length effigy of the ex-jester, who ended his unusual career as prior of the church he had founded. The sculpture captures everything that you would expect of a godly man. Hands clasped in prayer, he is the very model of piety, dignity and deep seriousness. Yet once a comic, always a comic. To underline this message, a little carved figure cavorts at the top of the canopy. It is a miniature jester.

One real-life personage of medieval London leads the field in terms of enduring, unabated merriment. Sir Richard Whittington might have been surprised, even shocked, to find himself the central figure in a knockabout romp, even one as beloved as *Dick Whittington and his Cat*. But it has ensured him immortality. How many other names from the list of London's 761 Lord Mayors can anybody call to mind?

Above left: A detail from Rahere's tomb. The little stone jester perched on the central pilaster plays sly tribute to the great churchman's original job.

Above right: Prior William Bolton's oriel window, an interior feature of the Church of St Bartholomew the Great, was allegedly commissioned by the church's boss, Rahere's successor, so that he could keep a beady eye on the behaviour of the monks below. True or not, there seems to be a deliberate air of playfulness about it. In the centre of the lower decorative moulding is an example of a rebus, or visual pun, playing on Bolton's name – a crossbow bolt shot through a tun (barrel).

Statue of Dick Whittington in Guildhall Yard. Legend says that Dick made his first fortune as a rat catcher. At this stage, he clearly had to find his form as a rodent operative. Unnoticed by either Dick or his cat, a rat is peeking out from behind the cat's tail.

The real-life Whittington was a well-born gentleman who rose to be a powerful banker, a gifted administrator and a charitable benefactor on an impressive scale. He did indeed achieve the distinction of being thrice Lord Mayor of London, a record still unchallenged, but otherwise his life and career hardly look like promising material for a pantomime. And nobody would ever have dared to refer to him as 'Dick'.

Legends around Dick Whittington – the lure of the streets paved with gold, the cat, the bells of St Mary Bow ringing 'turn again Whittington' – began to accrue in the early seventeenth century. They start to acquire a comic aspect, thanks to no less a figure than Mr Punch. In 1711, *The Spectator* announced that Punch would be taking the lead in 'an Entertainment' in Covent Garden piazza 'called, The History of Sir Richard Whittington, shewing his Rise from a Scullion to be Lord-Mayor of London, with the Comical Humours of Old Madge, the jolly Chamber-maid'. Old Madge, or similar characters, became a regular comic fixture, and by the start of the next century she and her kind had transferred to the pantomime stage, eclipsing the title character, and became the real stars of the show. The greatest of all clowns, Joe Grimaldi (see pp. 39–40), starred as the panto dame in Dick Whittington, taking the name Dame Cecily Suet. Since then, this tale of Old London has formed a staple of every British Christmas. And nobody has ever been able to hear the name of the illustrious Lord Mayor Sir Richard Whittington – a dignified, vastly wealthy and powerful figure to whom even kings deferred – without cracking a smile.

Puns thrived in medieval London, then as now. St Mary-le-Bow church, the site of London's largest bakery, supplied bread to all parts of the city. It was widely known as St Mary-le-Dough. The picture shows the ancient church before its destruction in the Great Fire of London. In the foreground is Cheapside Cross, destroyed by Puritan iconoclasts in 1643.

As medieval castles go, the Tower of London has led a surprisingly peaceful existence. The city's greatest medieval monument has never been besieged or witnessed significant conflict of any kind. Its most enduring function has been that of visitor attraction, a role played for almost half of its 960-year existence. Britain's first public museum opened here in the 1660s. Since then, the only people threatening to overrun the Tower have been tourists. Humorists of every stripe have rejoiced in the discrepancy between the Tower's grim reputation and its mostly homely reality. This cartoon postcard, by the great master of double entendre Donald McGill, is one of many to make play with the word 'bloody' (as in Bloody Tower), a word once considered highly shocking.

"Can you direct me to the – er – adjective tower?"

4

Superstars, Satire and Censorship, 1577–1660

Comedy was not exactly invented in Tudor London, but it did assume a new guise. Humour, for the first time, was turned into a cash-on-the-nail business. Londoners had always found ways to laugh, but now they turned over at least some of the process to professionals.

Groups of travelling players had been banging on London's gates for decades. The city was packed with would-be punters, as eager to enjoy comedy as the players were keen to perform to them. London also offered the prospect of patronage, fame and glory, although its inhabitants could not, at that stage, have imagined the full cosmic extent of the glory that was about to descend, courtesy of a certain country boy newly arrived from Stratford-upon-Avon.

For many years they banged in vain. The city fathers, smugly ensconced behind the old city walls, were flatly opposed to anything in the way of permanent theatres. One Lord Mayor, Sir Ambrose Nicholas, described playhouses as meccas for 'vagrant persons, masterless men, thieves and horse-stealers, utterlie past all shame'.

Undeterred, the travelling players closed in, reaching ever closer to the London heartland as the years passed. They could stroll into the city, just like anyone else, but only as real-life figures in a crowd, not as performers in make-believe land. In the meantime, the urge to set up a permanent home led to one of the great real-life jokes of English theatre history. This was nothing less than a theatre (London's very first) masquerading as an inn, The Red Lion. No doubt it served a few quarts of ale along the way, but performance art was The Red Lion's real stock in trade. Disguised behind the facade lay a 5ft-high stage, equipped with a fly-tower and trapdoors.

Based in unfashionable Whitechapel, The Red Lion appears to have disguised itself rather too well. It was not a success, either as a pub or a theatre. But ten years later, in 1577, James Burbage, carpenter and entrepreneur, openly challenged the authorities by constructing a permanent playhouse, just outside the City of London's walls, in Shoreditch. For a title, he chose an ancient Greek word that had been virtually obsolete for centuries – Theatre. Nobody tried to close it down. Londoners, fashionable and filthy alike, flocked to see Burbage's productions, and the genie was well and truly uncorked. The Theatre marked the dawn of full-time professional entertainment in London. Other theatres were built to satisfy the mass demand. They dodged the city authorities by building on the

The site in Stepney Way, Whitechapel, of the curious, short-lived hybrid known as The Red Lion, constructed around 1566 (see p. 20). The position is now occupied by another ex-hostelry, The Old Artichoke, once an East End institution and famous for its comedy singers, but closed since 2001. The Royal London Hospital stands at the end of the road.

South Bank, also (just) outside the bureaucratic control of the killjoys. Southwark, prefix notwithstanding, effectively became the first West End. The theatrical dawn swiftly turned into a heyday.

The most popular genre was comedy. Indeed, playgoers' appetite for a good laugh meant that they would sniff out comic material in the most unpromising places. The tragedian Thomas Dekker wrote crossly that London crowds would 'laugh aloud in the middle of the saddest scene of the terriblest tragedy'. Shakespeare may well have been thinking of London audiences when he wrote of 'overdone' material that 'though it makes the unskillful laugh, cannot but make the judicious grieve'.

London stage comedy began to develop a character of its own, drawing its special flavour from the vitality of the streets. In the process, of course, they added to, and became a key part of, that life force in its own right.

Far from seeking escapism, London audiences liked to see their own lives reflected on stage. Just two years after The Theatre opened its doors, the acerbic social commentator Stephen Gosson visited this playhouse and afterwards wrote, 'it is a right comedy to mark their appearance'. He was referring not to the performers but the audience. These knew what to expect from comedies with titles like *A Chaste Maid in Cheapside, Bartholomew Fair* (referring to London's largest annual fair, held in Smithfield), *The Weeding of Covent*

Middle Temple Hall lies between Fleet Street and the Embankment. The first recorded performance of Shakespeare's enchanting comedy *Twelfth Night* took place here on Candlemas night, 1602, a last burst of fun at the end of the twelve days of Christmas.

Garden, The Merry Devil of Edmonton and *The Isle of Dogs*. Works like these are packed, sometimes almost to excess, with references to familiar locations. Among the most common references are to Tottenham Court Road, where fashionable ladies resorted to enjoy cream syllabubs and other desserts provided by the cows grazing on Moor Fields; to Pannier Alley, where basketware shops and bakers sat side by side, feeding off each other's trade; to Budge Row, the furriers' centre; to the 'Straits of Bermuda', the narrow alleyways off Charing Cross, where citizens had to run a gauntlet of layabouts, cadging tobacco and money for strong drink; and, with notable frequency, to Turnmill Street, the north-of-the-river brothel quarter, supposedly much patronised by clergy from nearby St Paul's Cathedral. Although scenery in the sense of painted backdrops, or flats, was not in use, the stages weren't entirely bare. Trade signs, such as The Pig's Head (cooked meats) or The Bush (a gin tavern), were regularly used as on-stage props, helping to further implant the sense of an actual London street.

The new world of professional comedy opened up great opportunities for fame and fortune. It resulted in the emergence of a previously unknown breed, the celebrity comic. Within a few years of the opening of The Theatre, the city resounded to names like Richard Tarlton, Will Kempe, Robert Armin and Lawrence Fletcher, all of them alumni of the monarch's own professional troupe, The Queen's Men. These were Britain's first showbiz legends. Their fame can be gauged by the number of broadsheet ballads, complete with crude portraits, that were penned about them. The wealth they accumulated is revealed in their wills. They even achieved relative respectability, a word not previously associated with strolling players. A couple of comic actors were appointed Grooms of the Queen's Chamber.

Individuals had their particular stock-in-trade. For instance, John Adams, of The Queen's Men, perfected a long-running act based on flea infestation. He stole many a show by capering around the stage, scratching wildly.

Probably the most-famous specialty act was that of Will Kempe, whose dances were a complete comedy narrative in themselves, often very bawdy ones. Kempe has been immortalised by his epic nine-day, almost non-stop dance from London to Norfolk. The stunt was treated like the journey of an Olympic torch and attended by huge crowds along the way. Shakespeare may have had Kempe in mind when he rants about pushy clowns and any ad-libbing funnyman who makes a takeover bid on the show. 'Let those that play your clowns speak no more than is set down for them.'

Theatregoing was not the most popular of pastimes in Tudor London. Top of the pops came bull and bear baiting. Maybe the cruelty and bloodshed got a bit heavy, even for the tastes of Tudor audiences, because they were intercut with odd comedy sessions, in which

Sir John Falstaff, arguably Shakespeare's most outstanding comic creation. The 'Fat Knight', companion to young Prince Hal (the future Henry V), carouses his way through *The First Part of King Henry IV, The Second Part of King Henry IV* and *The Merry Wives of Windsor*. Some of his funniest escapades are set in The Boar's Head, Eastcheap, demolished during construction south of the Bank of England.

The Elizabethan Bear Garden, Bankside, constructed close to and around the same time as the Globe Theatre of Shakespearean fame. Bloodsports, such as bull and bear baiting, were interspersed with bouts of robust comedy.

humans became the bait. The German traveller Leopold von Wedel recalled watching one of these farces at a South Bank bullring in 1585. A giant model of a rose was set in the middle of the ring. Groups of London beggars and recipients of the Poor Rate (all no doubt starving) were positioned around the giant flower. Suddenly, the petals of the rose opened out, and piles of apples, pears and buns tumbled onto the ground. As the beggars stooped to grab the food, they were shot from behind with rockets and other fireworks. Unsurprisingly, the beggars capered around howling with pain and fear, which 'caused great amusement to the spectators'.

Not all animal acts were as cruel as bear baiting. One noted celebrity about town in Tudor London was Bartelmy, an ape. Bartelmy was a regular comedy star at fairgrounds, and it was said that he had also performed at the court of Queen Elizabeth I. He would respond to different words or actions in ways that caused mass hilarity to observers. Mention Spain, England's great enemy, or the Puritan, who wanted to close down all theatres and other forms of performance, and Bartelmy would blow a raspberry. Gallants would present their lady companions to Bartelmy. Overwhelmed by their beauty, the ape would prostate himself in front of the fabulous females. Present him with someone less desirable, however, and Bartelmy would cover his eyes.

The period between the execution of King Charles I in 1649 and the Restoration of the monarchy in 1660 was one of the most remarkable in the history of London humour, because there wasn't any – not officially, in any case.

Londoners laughed a lot when they attended the theatre, and often they were laughing at Puritanism. Malvolio in *Twelfth Night*, pompous, overbearing and utterly without any sense of absurdity, is identified as a Puritan by his boss, Maria. So, at the start of the English Civil War in 1642, with the Puritans firmly in charge of the city, all London theatres were closed down by special ordinance. The reason given was simple. Audiences laughed. London theatres, according to the preamble to the ordinance, encouraged 'lascivious Mirth and Levity'.

Over-elaborate Elizabethan male costume, and the foppish mannerisms that went with it, were a regular butt of London wits. Shakespeare has Falstaff promise: 'I will devise matter enough ... to keep Prince Harry in continual laughter the wearing out of six fashions'. (Detail from *Malvolio and the Countess* by Daniel Maclise, The National Gallery)

Of course, the result was that humour simply went underground. Cromwellian London abounded with muffled sniggers. Oliver Cromwell himself became the butt of many subversive jokes. The great Protector's name was pronounced Crumwell at the time. In covert Royalist taverns, such as The Red Bull of Clerkenwell, a coded grace was recited at mealtimes. 'God send this *crumb well* down.' The canard that Cromwell was henpecked by his wife, and a martyr to her awful cooking, provided further ammunition. According to one story, Cromwell was confronted at dinner with a particularly slimy and foul-smelling lump of fatty meat, devoid of any sauce or dressing. He requested an orange, to squeeze over the meat. 'I will not have oranges in the house,' barked his wife. 'Not with oranges at four pence a pound in the Convent market.' Four pence in the pound was the sum exacted on the wealth of some of the King's supporters as a financial penalty.

So, humour survived, albeit in a less upfront form. And even the Lord Protector himself was not beyond the odd guffaw. When some 'Popish' (i.e. ornate Catholic) vestments, confiscated from Jesuit priests, were shown to him, Cromwell ordered his attendants to dress up in them, 'causing abundance of mirth'.

With the Restoration of the monarchy in 1660, humour, so long suppressed, exploded like a streamer bomb at a party. In an act replete with symbolism, the body of the writer Thomas May was disinterred from its grave in Westminster Abbey's Poets' Corner and tossed into a pit. May had begun his literary career writing comedies. Then, after the execution of Charles I, he switched modes and wrote pamphlets in praise of Oliver Cromwell. His empty grave was reserved for another humorist, the Restoration wit and impresario William Davenant, eventually buried there in 1668. Humour trumped seriousness, even in death.

Above: The site of The Red Bull, Clerkenwell, known throughout its existence as the bad boy of London theatres. Developed out of a tavern, it specialised in raucous comedies and was a byword both for subversion and rowdiness. During the Cromwellian period, it was a haunt of Royalists and a source of anti-Parliamentary lampoons that circulated through London. It was demolished in the early nineteenth century to make way for Nicholson's Brewery. Hayward's Place, pictured, is thought to follow the line of the theatre's main passageway. The cottages were constructed to house brewery workers.

Left: The Aldersgate site of the seventeenth-century Rutland House, framed by a portion of the Brutalist Barbican development. This is where a resourceful jape inadvertently made artistic history. During the Commonwealth period under Oliver Cromwell (1649–60), theatre performances of any kind were prohibited. Musicmaking was also banned in public places but permitted in private residences. To bypass the laws, playwright and impresario William Davenant staged a work called *The Siege of Rhodes* at his private residence, Rutland House. Termed a 'music recital' to hoodwink the censors, the 1656 production is recognised as the first ever staging of an opera in Britain.

5

From Merry England to Wits' End, 1660–1837

In the years following the Restoration of the monarchy in 1660, Londoners were allowed to laugh again. Merriment was unleashed. The new king, Charles II, immediately acquired the soubriquet 'the merry monarch'. If good cheer had been suppressed throughout the years of Cromwellian rule, it now became pretty well obligatory. The scale of merriment can be gauged by the great chronicle of the period, Samuel Pepys's diary, where the word 'merry' abounds to the point of incontinence.

In the heady atmosphere of the time, the simplest stimulus could induce an outburst of mirth. For instance, 'had two mince pies ... and so we were very merry'. This atmosphere of merriment was fostered from the top. King Charles certainly had his shortcomings, debauchery, laziness and duplicity to name but three. Nobody, though, could ever describe him as a mournful presence. His perambulations were accompanied by swirls and trails of laughter, and he had a knack for disarming potentially tense moments by using humour.

One of Charles II's first acts following his accession was a direct command that the theatres should reopen. In terms of the sheer number of plays written and produced

St Paul's Church, Covent Garden, commissioned in 1633 and known ever since as 'the actor's church'. Funerals and memorial services for members of the acting profession have traditionally been held here. Commemorative plaques inside the church include ones to 'legends of London comedy', including Charlie Chaplin, Barbara Windsor, Nicholas Parsons, Stanley Holloway, Richard Briers, June Whitfield, Hattie Jacques, Brian Rix and Bernard Cribbins. The plaques inspired a short verse credited to a number of disconsolate actor managers: 'The play's a flop, the curtain falls/On another failed endeavour/But hope awaits on the walls of St Pauls/Where the show goes on forever.'

The Punch & Judy pub, in the Covent Garden covered market, situated opposite the Church of St Paul's. It is named in honour of a memorable day. An entry in Samuel Pepys's 1662 diary mentions a puppet show, enacted under cover of the church's imposing portico – the first ever record of a Punch & Judy performance.

Samuel Pepys's bust is mounted on the site of his London home, with modern Seething Lane in the background. The great diarist (and high-ranking government official) remained here in London throughout the terrible plague of 1665. Most of his neighbours in Seething Lane perished from the disease. Sam attributed his survival to the medical effects of perpetual laughter. He adhered to the widespread belief that mirth could stop the bubonic plague in its tracks, along with the audacity to put this conviction to the test.

in London, the years following the 1660 Restoration proved to be probably the most productive in the capital's theatrical history. The bulk of these works, reflecting the merry monarch's own taste, were comedies. Once again, Londoners flocked to the theatre for laughter. And across the land, amateur theatricals re-erupted.

Out of this torrent of thespian mirth emerged a new being, the comedienne. Female performers were not only licensed for the first time to appear on stage, but they were also free to make audiences roar with laughter. This they did with aplomb. In the reign of the merry monarch, a number of comedy actresses became famous, rich and royal mistresses, though not necessarily in that particular order. One of this bunch has passed into folklore.

Nell Gwynn, a lowly Londoner raised in a brothel, had little success playing straight parts on stage. But given the chance to demonstrate her talent in comic roles, she became the toast of the town. In one play, she delivered her lines directly to the audience: 'I know you in your hearts hate serious plays, as I do serious parts.' The words were spoken straight from Nell's soul.

Yet the easy merriment was not unadulterated. It was infiltrated by slivers of much darker humour. During the Parliamentary period, humour had gone underground, and although it was freed up by the return of the monarchy in 1660, it retained its sense of a guarded snigger. And during its Cromwellian troglodyte period, humour had also evolved into a form that London had seen little of before. Satire.

A 1904 cartoon depicting the legendary, although probably fictitious, first encounter between Charles II and his mistress Nell Gwynn. Nell is said to have accosted the king, tried to sell him an orange and ended up with a more lucrative deal. In fact, the pair probably met as a result of Nell's celebrity as a comedic actress. This didn't stop Nell from milking the orange-selling legend for all it was worth.

"THE COMIC HISTORY OF ENGLAND." *After designs by S. H. Hebblethwaite.*
NELL GWYNNE AND CHARLES II. As Nell said, "She would never have known it was the King (him being so affable) if her young brother hadn't tipped her the wink!"

Nell Gwynn House, a luxury apartment block in Sloane Avenue, occupies the site of 'the little Chelsea cottage' where Nell lived and where she entertained a significant proportion of London society. Nell's legend spread beyond her native shores. In the 1880s, a comic opera by a French composer, titled simply *Nell Gwynn*, played in theatres around Europe.

A perky statue of Nell Gwynn, set into the facade of Nell Gwynn House, depicts the legendary comedienne in her most famous pose – selling oranges. The little dog at her feet is a Cavalier King Charles Spaniel, a sly reference to Nell's best-known lover.

The relaxed regime of Charles II unleashed the satirists, and there was no lack of material for them. As far as the royal court was concerned, it rapidly became clear that 'merry' was a euphemism for rumpy pumpy. Whispers of this had reached Sam Pepys within a few weeks of the coronation, and he was soon in despair. The reign that had begun with such excited anticipation soon degenerated into rebellious anger and a political divisiveness that threatened to unseat the monarchy for a second time. But for satirists, it was manna from heaven.

Heading up these satirists was John Dryden, the first Poet Laureate. As such, he had a front row seat from which to observe the excesses of London high society. Despite being the recipient of royal patronage, Dryden had no hesitation in biting the hand that fed him. His stage comedy *Amphitryon*, for instance, uses a tale from Greek mythology as a vehicle for a scarcely disguised tilt at the prevailing sexual free-for-all. In the play *Jupiter*, king of the gods – a direct portrait of King Charles II – sets out to seduce the wife of the triumphant general Amphitryon. In pursuit of his wicked way, Jupiter adopts the appearance of Amphityron, while conspiring to keep the genuine article from returning home. However, even a chief god's plans can go awry, and the real Amphityron arrives home at the worst possible time for Jupiter. Farcical chaos then erupts as not one but two lust-crazed Amphitryons rampage around the bedroom door. The disguise doesn't fool Jupiter's wife, Juno, and once hubby is back in the skies, the queen of the gods starts hurling stars at his head.

The statue of Queen Anne in front of the portico of St Paul's Cathedral. Poor Queen Anne had a widespread reputation, and it wasn't for churchgoing. The loss of all eighteen of her children, plus the painful effects of gout, were said to have driven her to the brandy bottle. Noting the odd alignment of the statue and the direction of its gaze, the town wits came up with the lines: 'Brandy N'Anne, Brandy N'Ann/It's the wrong way you perch/You're facing the gin shop/Your back's to the church.'

St George's Church, Bloomsbury, built at enormous expense as a symbol of the link between Church and State, and the right of the House of Hanover to the British Crown. To drive home the point, it is topped not by a cross but by the statue of much-despised King George I. Horace Walpole wrote mockingly: 'When Henry VIII left the pope in the lurch/He ruled over England as head of the church/But George's good subjects, the Bloomsbury people/Instead of the church made him head of the steeple.'

Even as audiences flocked to see the play, Dryden fell prey to the old satirist's despair. How could humorous satire, however wild, ever match the craziness of real life? 'Satire's ... sharp sting is gone ... We would laugh, but cannot find the jest,' he lamented.

The Restoration coincided with (possibly triggered) an explosive expansion. By 1700, London had become the largest city in the world, indeed, the largest ever seen on the face of the globe. The building frenzy gave rise to a new English word, 'jerry-built', taken from a character in Samuel Foote's 1764 stage farce *The Mayor of Garratt*.

If the authorities were discombobulated, so were London's creative folk. This new and unprecedented landscape, Europe's first true urban jungle, growing up at warp speed around them, made their head spin and their stomachs heave. One way to cope was with satirical humour.

The London effect as it hit one country boy, arriving in the great city for the first time, proved almost overwhelming. In March 1737, the young Samuel Johnson walked from his home in the quiet, respectable cathedral city of Lichfield, bent on making his fortune in the capital. After a few horrified days' exposure to this Gotham, he very nearly hightailed it home again. Instead, however, he settled on another way to respond. He wrote a poem entitled, simply, 'London'. This is the first published work from the man who was to become the arch Londoner. The citizen who would one day opine 'when a man is tired of London

The statue of Dr Samuel Johnson, perhaps England's greatest man of letters, presides over Fleet Street, 'the street of ink and adventure'. Johnson's repartee inspired his friend and biographer James Boswell to write: 'In London one may laugh in as many (different) ways as one speaks.'

he is tired of life', began his writing career with an all-out moralist's blast at the depravity of the city, the collapse of its infrastructure and its godawful inhabitants. Unlike other sober moralists, however, Sam Johnson was wise enough to recognise that humour was a more powerful weapon than po-faced preachiness. 'London', the poem, is a laugh-out-loud depiction of the city, which juxtaposes the exaggeratedly awful and the simply ridiculous:

> Their ambush here relentless ruffians lay
> And here the fell attorney prowls for prey.
> Here falling houses thunder on your head
> And here a female atheist talks you dead.

Restoration and eighteenth-century society retained a huge relish for verbal wordplay. The satirists were masters at making words dance, and some of their choicest couplets were directed at the fast-changing London cityscape, along with the innate symbolism of some of the new buildings.

Christopher Wren's Monument to the Great Fire of London, completed in 1677, featured a stone tablet which blamed the conflagration on a wholly imaginary Roman Catholic conspiracy. The spurious words were chiselled away at the time of Catholic emancipation

A political cartoon by James Gillray depicts *The Wits of the Age Setting the Table in a Roar.* A gathering of London's most-celebrated mirthmongers, feasting on port and oysters, roars with laughter at its own bon mots. The table around which they are gathered stands for the country at large, and the message is clear. Wit ruled, OK. In the Restoration and Hanoverian periods, it was a powerful force that could make or break a man.

in 1830, but Alexander Pope, himself a Catholic, had already levelled the Monument with two lines of caustic wit, referring to: 'Where London's column, pointing at the skies/Like a tall bully, lifts the head, and lies.'

London's satirists viewed their city with a jaundiced eye. Yet alongside the chaos and corruption there boomed an altogether brighter London. London was fast outstripping Paris to become the most-confident, prosperous and, above all, artistically creative city in the Western hemisphere. Sam Johnson swiftly came to recognise this brighter side. Even his opinion of its jokes improved.

New ways were emerging all the time. As the seventeenth century moved into its final years, the tenor of London humour changed. 'Merry' had been the keynote of Restoration London. It was gradually ousted by a different notion. London became 'the realm of wit'.

Witticisms became almost an alternative currency. A man could rise to fame and power on the back of a well-tuned tongue. 'We ought to have a great dread of the power of these terrible men,' wrote Thomas Sprat in his *History of the Royal Society*. A suggestion was even made (possibly as an attempt at wit itself) that the monarch should commission a series of portraits of the greatest wits at court to be hung in Whitehall Palace. One councillor took the suggestion seriously, advising that 'would not the rest think that [the King] called them fooles?'

The social history of the era can be navigated via its jokes. The wits always had an eye for new trends and hot topics, and great kudos attached to anyone who could produce a witty comment on the latest news or fad to hit town. Alexander Pope, ever a specialist at hitting two targets with one poetic couplet, soared to top of the wit parade when he wrote about one of the great social phenomena of the age: coffee. The first coffee house was opened in London in 1652, and by the 1720s they had become an established feature of London life as the focal point of news, gossip and networking. Some, however, including Pope, took a bleak view of coffee. With a few choice words he speared both the beverage and the race of Whitehall politicians when he wrote, 'Coffee, which makes the politician wise/And see through all things with his half-shut eyes.'

In a window in an alleyway off Cornhill stands a vintage urn, proclaiming the site of London's first coffee house. These lively venues were central to the city's witticism network. A morning's amusing remark would flash around the 'coffee circuit' and could make the man who uttered it famous within twenty-four hours.

The medieval St John's Gatehouse in Clerkenwell was the site of Hogarth's, a coffee house run by the father of the artist William Hogarth. Its proprietor claimed that it was the venue of choice for the finest-honed wits in London, attracted there by House Rule No.1 – conversation could only be conducted in the 'noble classical languages'. The coffee house wits mocked this claim. One wrote: 'Doctors and Schollars now meet where the folk do speak/Nought of language but Latin & Greek/Passing prentice-boys/And low Hobdehois (tongue-tied youths)/Do marvel much/ At the strange noise.'

The coffee houses acted as amplifiers for the town wits (this may partly explain Pope's hostility to them, since they were rivals in the humour stakes). A *bon mot* launched upon the world at a London soirée one evening would be passed by word of mouth across the coffee cups the next morning. Evening would see it quoted in clubs and at dinner tables right across the capital. By the end of the week, it would have appeared in print in numerous London journals and newspapers. The process brought a whole new meaning to the term quick wit.

Politicians, naturally, latched onto wit power. The era's most potent demagogue, John Wilkes, used wit as a political tool. His witticisms became so famous with the public at large that they often overshadowed the cause (universal suffrage) they were supposed to advance. Charles Johnson, Wilkes's friend, said of the great freedom fighter, 'he would sacrifice his best friend for the sake of a scurvy jest'. In later life, Wilkes made the shift from people's champion to conservative establishment figure, even rising to become Lord Mayor of London. But the wit remained till the last. According to Benjamin Franklin, betting men took a wager that may be unique in London history. During his tenure as Lord Mayor, Wilkes would walk every morning from his home in the West End to the Guildhall.

Along the way, he was stopped by many people seeking his help or merely wanting to shake his hand. The wager was that not one of these people came away from the encounter without laughing.

Along with the verbal wit, Georgian London also experienced a golden age, if it can be called that, of practical joking. This zest for physical japes came out of nowhere and lasted through to the age of Bertie Wooster (p. 83). An early and famous practitioner of this art form was the dramatist Richard Brinsley Sheridan, who relished dramatic comedy in his own life as well as in his stage plays. On one occasion, Sheridan put the word about town that he was at death's door. A long line of London's great and good lined up at his bedside to say their farewells. Sheridan's friend, the Prince of Wales, said that he realised Sheridan was 'bound for the graveyard' when the playwright refused to drink a glass of the finest claret.

Sheridan knew that one of the major balls of the season was set to take place. Rising from his 'deathbed', he caked himself in white stage make-up and wrapped himself in coffin sheets. He then made a grand entrance to the ball. The arrival of this walking corpse caused 'gentlemen as well as ladies to faint, and many glasses to be broken'. Sheridan's friends knew their man better. 'Glad to see you've made a full recovery, Sheridan,' said the politician and diarist Thomas Creevey.

Another dedicated practical joker was the young Scots aristocrat James Boswell, later the companion and biographer of Dr Samuel Johnson. In contrast to Sheridan, Boswell's practical jokes had a tendency to go badly wrong.

On a whim, and 'in a frolicsome humour', Boswell arranged a 'tickling party'. His friends the Temple brothers were invited to his rooms in Whitehall, where they were ambushed and tickled from top to bottom by some ladies hired by Boswell for the purpose. Boswell then joined in. Everyone giggled so much that the landlord thought an orgy was taking place on his premises and so he called the night watch. Boswell did not see the funny side. Indeed, he was so angry that he resolved to hand in his notice.

Even waxworks could indulge in practical buffoonery. Mrs Salmon's establishment in Fleet Street, the precursor to Madame Tussaud's, contained a waxwork of the prophetess Old Mother Shipton. But the wax statue was also an automaton. Visitors would examine the statue, turn their backs – and Old Mother Shipton would promptly kick them in the bottom.

The theatre boomed, as ever, among all classes of society (when ticket prices were raised in 1809, riots spread across the capital). The period gave rise to a great comedy star in the shape of Samuel Foote, the first ever professional impressionist. Foote was certainly no man of the people. He was the son of an MP and a gentleman of independent means (Samuel had inherited a fortune from one of his uncles who had been murdered by another uncle).

Foote aspired to be a great Shakespearian tragic actor but found his legs in comedy roles. Or rather leg, for he had lost one of his limbs in a riding accident. His artificial leg became a famous comic prop, but it was for his mimicry that Foote became famous. Quick to recognise the box office appeal of funny voices, Foote turned his supposedly straight stage roles into exercises in inspired parroting. He claimed to be able to reproduce any voice in London after hearing it just once. 'He had such wonderful powers of mimicry,' it was said, 'that even his victims fell into helpless laughter'. Like other comics, Foote nursed a longing to play tragic parts. In the end, he wrote and staged his own tragedy, *The Orators*. But the laugh was on him. James Boswell, a regular victim of the blues, regarded Foote as a surefire antidote. After viewing *The Orators*, he records: 'There did I laugh ... very heartily'. After that, 'my gloom was gone'.

For the most part, theatreland's characters and plots were drawn from so-called polite society. Whether in the gods or the stalls, audiences craved rich costumes, fine furniture and high-flown language. Yet they also discovered an appetite for low-life comedy. This was proved, sensationally, by the success of *The Beggar's Opera*, the most popular stage production of the entire eighteenth century. The cast was made up of thieves, fences and gaolers. And it was this underclass that could claim to have developed an entire new category of humour.

On the site of modern-day Marble Arch stood the London gallows. Down the decades, a steady stream of offenders, including many children, streamed west from the gates of Newgate gaol, along the Oxford Road (now Oxford Street), for the rendezvous with 'Tyburn Tree'.

The Angel Inn, St Giles High Street. Condemned prisoners on the way to the Tyburn gallows would stop at the hostelry to enjoy a bowl of 'nut brown ale and strong spirits'. The tavern came to be known, for obvious reasons, as the Halfway House. It was also nicknamed The Pay on the Nail, since it was, for obvious reasons, the only pub in London where the landlord never, ever, offered credit to passing trade. Known for a while, officially, as The Bowl, the inn reverted to its original, medieval name when rebuilt in 1873.

Great premium was attached to the notion of going merrily to one's death, and it was along the Oxford Road that the notion of gallows humour developed. One condemned man 'caused great mirth among the onlookers' when it started to drizzle, and he demanded an umbrella. Jack Sheppard marked his path to execution by stopping for noggins of sack along the way. Daniel Defoe, who reported on the event, said that he continually burst into laughter.

In Tyburn gallows humour, we hear the humour of the low-life taverns, the brothels, the thieves' dens and the slum alleyways. John Gay tapped into this for *The Beggar's Opera.* Theatrical comedy generally was more high flown. But from London's poverty quarters there emerged a giant figure, a comic colossus who made the whole population, rich and poor alike, rock with laughter. This was Grimaldi, perhaps the greatest of all clowns and certainly the most famous within his own lifetime.

Joe Grimaldi was the first professional funnyman since the Elizabethan period to become a household name, the first to find a lustre matching that of the other A-list celebrities of the day, the statesmen and military and naval heroes. A measure of his stature was that he gained a biographer even more illustrious than himself. After Grimaldi's death, Charles Dickens completed the clown's unfinished memoirs. For Dickens, the project was personal. As a boy, he had seen The Great Grimaldi on stage at Chatham and would never forget the tide of 'glorious, unstoppable laughter' that flowed from the audience – and himself.

A story told by Dickens in the book testifies to the near veneration which Londoners showed Grimaldi. At the height of his fame, Grimaldi was booked to appear regularly in two different theatres on the same night, Sadler's Wells and Covent Garden (this was a common practice for London performers). A coach stood waiting for him at the Islington stage door. As soon as Grimaldi had finished his Sadler's Wells stint, and still dressed in his clown's costume, he would dive into the coach.

He would then be carried at breakneck speed from Clerkenwell to Covent Garden, invariably arriving with just minutes to spare.

The notorious thief, escapee and popular hero Jack Sheppard enjoys his final drink at the Halfway House. According to Daniel Defoe, great gusts of laughter followed Sheppard 'all the way to the gallows'. Sheppard himself joked: 'I cannot stir ... into the country ... but they [the public] are all at my heels laughing after me.' (William Harold Amos)

One night, the coach failed to arrive and no other transport was available. 'In an agony of fear', knowing that his non-appearance at Covent Garden would cause a riot, he set off to run from Islington to the West End.

But a man running through the streets in full clown's costume was scarcely going to pass unnoticed. The distinctive make-up of this particular clown was soon recognised, and the cry went up: 'Here's Joe Grimaldi.'

By the time the great man reached Holborn, a crowd of several hundred was running with him. 'Suddenly,' by Dickens's account, 'he gave one of his famous and well-known laughs.' The crowd immediately formed a spontaneous bodyguard to clear the streets and allow Grimaldi fast access to the Covent Garden theatre.

Grimaldi also created a legacy that remains more powerful than ever in British theatre, and even perhaps the British identity. He was responsible for the Christmas panto as it now exists. The process started early in life. Joe first trod the stage as a child prodigy – a child with the blood of generations of popular performers in his ancestry. His early appearances were in so-called harlequinades, Londonised versions of the Italian *commedia dell'arte* tradition. They were referred to as pantomimes (from Latin *pantomimus*, meaning a mime actor or dancer). But they weren't pantos as anybody recognises them today. Grimaldi subverted these graceful but rather formal entertainments, turning them into raucous, earthy and very English comedy shows. He also introduced comic songs in the style of the music hall, the new type of popular entertainment which was fast evolving in parallel with pantomime.

Members of the public mob the coach of superstar Joe Grimaldi. Even without his clown's make-up on, 'Joey' was instantly recognisable to Londoners.

Gradually, the influence of the purveyors of wit, privileged, sardonic and frequently decadent, as they were, began to fade. A new word, Victorian, set the tone for a new age. Clever cynicism became unfashionable.

In the world of comedy, Grimaldi, with his broader approach to humour, had led the charge. But for 'Joey', the man rather than the legend, the end was sad indeed. He came to personify the notion of the sad face and the weeping eye behind the clown's mask – a man worn out by his punishing performance schedule, crippled by a pratfall too far, broken in spirit by the death of his wife and son. The wits would have appreciated the irony of the sad funnyman, but by then they were all long gone themselves.

London didn't forget Grimaldi, but nor did it spend a lot of time weeping over his grave. It found other ways to laugh, because laughter, not melancholy, was the natural currency of London. It lasted from cradle to grave – and it didn't stop there. At least one great wit landed a grave in Westminster Abbey. The space came by way of thanks from a grateful nation for the laughter he had generated. Notified in advance of this accolade, John Gay, author of *The Beggar's Opera*, composed a two-line verse to adorn his gravestone. It applied to himself, it applied to Grimaldi and it is an appropriate rubric for those who work to make us laugh, in London and the world over. Today, abbey tour guides stop by Gay's memorial and read out these lines to their flock:

Life's a jest and all things show it,
I thought so once and now I know it.

The opening of the Royal Institution in 1799 heralded a new age of scientific advancement and rational thought. But its initial fame rested on a different role, as a centre of chemically induced laughter.

Visitors flocked to the Royal Institution's new building to experience the effects of 'laughing gas', developed and administered by the brilliant young scientist Humphrey Davy. Crowds then poured out onto Albermarle Street, hysterical with laughter. The resulting chaos led to an historic piece of town planning, when Albermarle Street was made into London's first official one-way thoroughfare.

6

We are Amused, 1837–1914

In July 1836, a meeting took place that was destined to change the way that London looked at and listened to itself, and the way the world saw London. The encounter was fictional, but its consequences in the real world proved historic.

This was the first meeting between Mr Sam Pickwick, perpetual president of the Pickwick Club, and Sam Weller, the cheery serving man who promptly became his comic companion and support. Together, Pickwick and Weller were destined to conquer the global imagination.

Opened in 1750, Westminster Bridge caused a sensation as the city's first to straddle the Thames since London Bridge in 1132. One summer morning, William Wordsworth took in the view from the bridge. The sight inspired the opening line of his sonnet: 'Earth hath not anything to show more fair.' The arches beneath rapidly became popular with those practising brass instruments thanks to the echo. Pedestrians were less delighted, leading to a parody of Wordsworth's poem which began: 'There's nothing on earth that looks more fair/Than Westminster Bridge in dawn's light/But on this thoroughfare, one must block each ear/For the sound ain't as good as the sight.'

One of Britain's quirkiest public statues is sited, incongruously, at the heart of a Croydon office complex. A huntsman crashes through a hedgerow in the heart of open countryside. The madcap rider is Jorrocks, cockney grocer and subject of a series of enduringly popular comic stories by R. S. Surtees, first published in the 1830s. Obsessed with 'the chase', Jorrocks was wont to gallop out from his City office, bound for the Surrey fields (where the offices now stand), in wild pursuit of foxes. The success of the Jorrocks stories, with their theme of Londoners adrift in rural England, led to the commissioning of *The Pickwick Papers*.

The coming together took place in the courtyard of the White Hart Inn, Southwark, close to the southern end of London Bridge, one of a cluster of ancient inns spread along Borough High Street (Chaucer's Tabard stood next door).

Mr Pickwick was the hero of *The Pickwick Papers*, a romp based on the mishaps of townee Londoners at large in the English countryside. It was published in monthly instalments, with the aim of eventually binding together all the episodes into a single illustrated volume.

The Pickwick Papers was originally conceived as a series of sporting prints by the leading illustrative artist Robert Seymour, with some accompanying text. No great significance was attached to the words; the publishers simply wanted a literary hack who would take his cue from the pictures and deliver the copy fast. They alighted on what seemed like the ideal candidate, a young parliamentary correspondent and roving journalist who was hoping to get married and was only too happy to earn a bit of extra cash. Neither the publishers nor Seymour recognised the force that they were about to unleash. They knew soon enough. Within weeks, Charles Dickens was calling the shots, the text was king, and the pictures mere illustrations of the storyline.

Even so, it took a while for *Pickwick* to go stratospheric. Hero he may have been, but Mr Pickwick wasn't doing too well at first. Sales were sluggish, until instalment

Charles Dickens's bust stands in the window of The George and Vulture with its back to Bengal Court, an alleyway unchanged since medieval times. Published in 1837, Dickens's comic novel *The Pickwick Papers* launched its young author into worldwide celebrity and soon had the world 'weeping with laughter in a dozen or more different languages'. The George and Vulture is a key *Pickwick Papers* location and remains exactly as Dickens knew it.

Sam Weller, loyal servant and perpetual wise guy, is depicted with his mail-coach driver father Tony in the courtyard of The White Hart Inn, Southwark. The meeting here of Sam and Mr Pickwick set the pair off on a series of fast-moving comic adventures which, as chronicled in *The Pickwick Papers*, captivated readers in every corner of the world. The White Hart was demolished in 1889.

The present-day site of the White Hart's yard, with the Shard in the background. It was one of a series of old galleried inn yards on the southern approach to London Bridge, of which only The George, owned by the National Trust, survives in its original form. These sites exert a powerful hold on London's comic imagination. A few yards to the south stood the real-life Tabard Inn (demolished 1873), location for the opening section of Chaucer's *Canterbury Tales.*

number ten. Then Sam Weller came along, and the trio of Pickwick, Weller and Dickens was in business. Almost overnight, the whole world was in love with *Pickwick.*

The two Sams between them had turned *The Pickwick Papers* from just another periodical publication into the most widely read work of English fiction to that date. The winning formula lay in the contrast between Mr Pickwick's naivety and Weller's worldliness, including an encyclopedic knowledge of London, which Sam Weller himself describes as 'extensive and peculiar'. Sam Weller also took over a big chunk of the English language. So called Wellerisms – platitudes shackled to case studies, tinged with black or cynical humour – started to pop up everywhere. An example from the book is: 'It's over and can't be helped, as they always says in Turkey, when they cuts the wrong man's head off.' By 1837, Wellerisms were ubiquitous in correspondence and diaries all over, and people were soon making up their own versions.

Sam Weller embodied something quite new in fiction: grassroots London humour. Cockney wit à la Weller must have been around for centuries, but until Dickens captured it in the shape of Sam, no one had actually tried to put it down on paper or even thought to do so. Indeed, one or two of Dickens's more snotty associates considered that he was demeaning himself by introducing a working-class character in a prime role. But the novelist, always supremely self-confident in his own giant vision, knew exactly what he was doing. Dickens wrote about what he knew, and what he knew was ordinary life and people. His own background was impeccably lower-middle class. His father was a naval pay-clerk.

The approach is captured in the sub-title to *Sketches by Boz*, the collection of Dickens's early short pieces, which preceded *The Pickwick Papers. Illustrative of Everyday Life and Everyday People* sounds bland enough, but it actually describes something altogether radical. Here were the clerks and landladies and shopkeepers, the cabmen and errand boys and sergeants of police and commercial travellers. They were the people whose vital energies powered London, an ancient city exploding in size and vigour under the effects of the Industrial Revolution. Such people had been despised, ignored or simply not noticed by previous social chroniclers of British life, such as, for all her virtues, Jane Austen. But they were the majority of the city's population. These humbler Londoners were embraced under the broad term 'cockney'. They were the underwater part of the London iceberg, the anonymous people who really powered the great city, that metropolis that both gave out and required energy in vast quantities.

LONDON going out of Town. — or — The March of Bricks & mortar! —

The breakneck expansion of London in the early nineteenth century is lampooned in an 1829 cartoon entitled *London Going Out of Town, or, The March of Bricks and Mortar.* Artist George Cruikshank's vision is both funny and unsettling. It shows a London kiln vomiting a great arc of bricks into the countryside, while a column of chimneys marches under its own steam in the same direction. Two haystacks flee for their lives, terrified trees pull up their own roots in a bid to escape the onslaught of bricks and mortar and a self-propelled wheelbarrow empties a mound of disgusting London refuse onto a once green and pleasant field.

A big element in that fuel was humour. Dickens cottoned on to the fact that these ordinary Londoners, like Sam, had a keen sense of the ridiculous. They joked, they mocked, they used laughter as a consolation for the hardships and drabness of their everyday life. This was the time when 'cockney humour' became a universally recognised term. 'If I were a humorist, I should most certainly be a Cockney humorist,' G. K. Chesterton wrote in 1909. 'All the best humour that exists in our language is Cockney humour.'

The popularity of Dickensian humour led a number of publishers to consider the notion of a weekly periodical devoted, entirely, to all things comical. There were a few failures, but in July 1841, a humorous journal was born, destined to become entrenched – so much so, that it was soon viewed as a symbol of British identity, essential study material for anyone who wanted to get to grips with the British character. Enter *Punch*.

Punch's tone was mellow and affable. It was devoted less to satire than the search for 'the eternal guffaw' (Dickens's not altogether complimentary words – as a radical, he was disappointed by *Punch*'s lack of political bite). Its original business prospectus painted it as a sort of social care institution for old jokes. It promised to be 'a refuge for destitute wit – an asylum for the thousands of orphan jokes ... the millions of perishing puns, which are now wandering about without so much as a shelf to rest upon'. It also promised to be a sort of journal of record, reporting humorous stories wherever its reporters found them.

The Punch Tavern in Fleet Street served for many years as the de facto editorial office of *Punch* magazine, the world's most celebrated humorous journal. Known originally as The Crown and Sugarloaf, the watering hole soon changed its name in honour of its most regular clients.

Punch drew on the whole, ever-widening, world for its humour, but in particular it observed life on its London doorstep. The magazine's founding editor, Mark Lemon, took long walks with his close family friend, Charles Dickens (him again). They learned to listen to conversations and exchanges in the street, in theatre foyers, at parties. They watched for trivial but comical incidents. The pair coined the term 'outs' to describe their haul of verbal and visual material, much of which, in due course, found its way into *Punch*'s weekly issue and into Dickens's novels. Countless anonymous Londoners contributed material for free, without realising it, simply by opening their mouths. One example will have to suffice.

1st down-and-out: ''Ad any breakfus' 's mornin'?'
2nd down-and-out: 'Not a drop.'

From *Punch*'s close-quarter observation of London everyday life, there also emerged one immortal fictional creation. This was Mr Pooter (see p. 57). The humble but smug

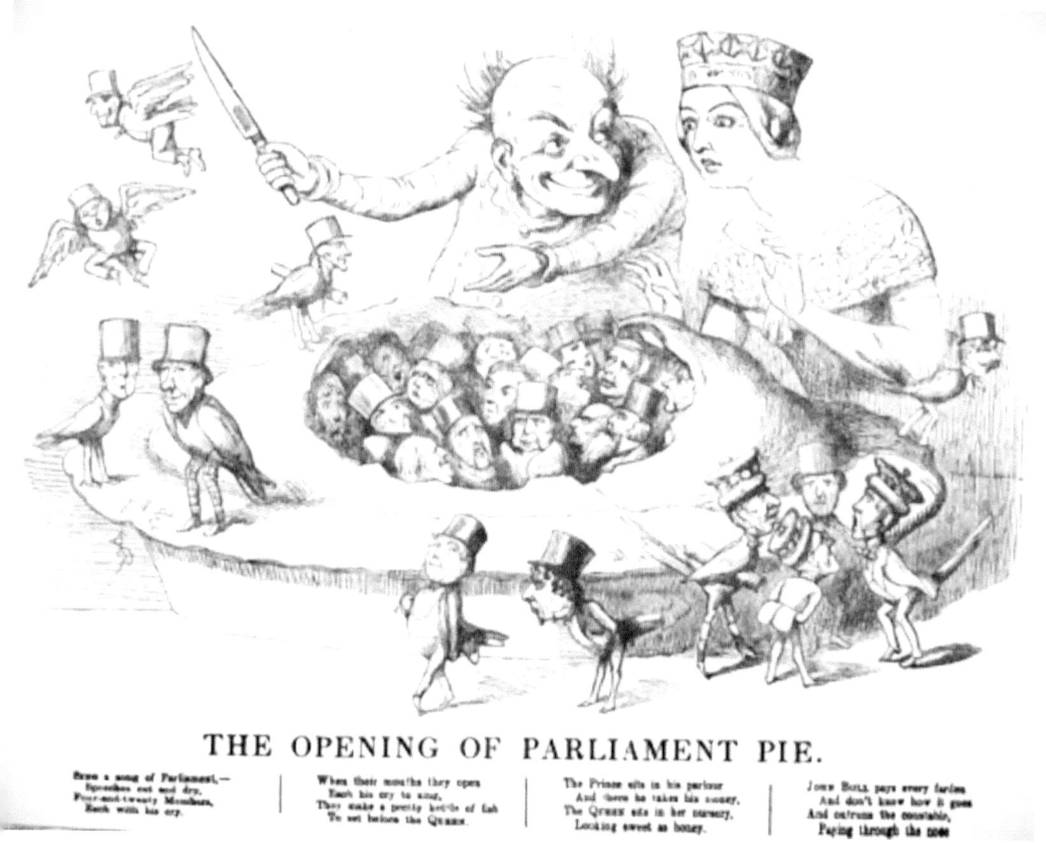

Punch magazine's humorous and exaggerated line drawings of parliament introduced a new usage into the English language – *cartoon.* The style was intended to express the silliness of parliamentary proceedings as viewed by *Punch*'s journalists and artists. Originally, the word cartoon applied to a very serious, preliminary sketch for a painting. Courtesy of *Punch,* it has come to be forever associated with humour.

insurance clerk was the brainchild of brother humorists George and Weedon Grossmith. His mild escapades were serialised in *Punch* between 1888 and 1889, before publication in book form as *The Diary of a Nobody*.

Dickens had given the London masses a voice, and that voice was now amplified via an exuberant new form of popular entertainment. The music hall soon loomed large across the nation, but it was developed in London.

Music hall had its roots in the song-and-supper rooms of Convent Garden, which flourished in the early decades of the nineteenth century. The most celebrated of these were the Coal Hole in the Strand and the Cider Cellars close by in Maiden Lane. Rowdy and raunchy, they were strictly men-only affairs. Professional or semi-pro singers would lead the lads in sing-songs, while the liquor flowed.

Come the new age of Victorian respectability, and gangs of moral guardians closed down the song and supper clubs. Their method was simple. They instituted a system of licensing, then refused to grant licences. The Puritans were also diligent in burning all the song sheets in an exercise of mass expurgation.

The supper-room songs were filthy, but they also aimed to be funny. The novelist William Thackeray was a regular attendee in his youth. He recalled, above all else, the 'really admirable, terrific humour'.

Victorian reformers shut down the song and supper rooms, but the Coal Hole spirit lived on in a revised format and on a whole new scale. A number of theatrical entrepreneurs had looked at the success of the low dives and recognised the opportunities for expansion, with far larger and more diverse audiences, bigger performing spaces and innuendo (which went over the moralists' heads) replacing total smut. A new term entered the language when The Grapes tavern in Southwark changed its name. By way of attracting those in search of a sing-song, but a clean and respectable one, it became the Grapes Music Hall.

In 1852, the impresario Charles Morton, subsequently dubbed 'the father of the halls', opened the first purpose-built music hall, the Canterbury, Westminster Bridge Road. Morton had himself been an enthusiastic participant in the defunct song and supper clubs. Always abuzz with groundbreaking brainwaves, he now put into practice the most radical of all his schemes. At the Canterbury he encouraged women to join the merrymaking, both as audience and performers.

The Canterbury was an overnight success. Within two years, Morton embarked on the construction of a much larger theatre. In order for the show to go on while rebuilding was in progress, the new music hall was constructed around the old Canterbury. Only when mark two was ready to receive the public was Canterbury mark one demolished. Simultaneously, the West End's first music hall, the Oxford in Oxford Street, rose on the site of the ancient Boar and Castle Inn. Now open to all, music hall quickly evolved into a mass entertainment and spread through the British Isles like a high-spirited invasion force.

Comedy lay at the core of music hall's appeal (counterpointed by a few more sentimental ditties). As the name music hall suggests, the humour was delivered through the medium of song. Stand-up humour did not evolve until the 1890s (the word comedian is first recorded in 1898). But audiences were more than happy to enjoy their humour in sung-through format.

The initial success of the Canterbury was largely down to its top-billed performer, Sam Cowell, the first of the great music hall stars. Sam's wife, Emilie, kept a diary in which

Right: London's first purpose-built music hall, the Canterbury, Westminster Bridge Road, pictured in 1849 at the time of its opening. Note the faint depiction of a steam train, top right. In reality, the Southern Railway viaduct ran within a few yards of the building.

Below: The forlorn site of the historic Canterbury music hall today. The building was destroyed by enemy action during the Blitz. Music hall memories aside, the footprint of the old theatre represents one of the last un-redeveloped bomb sites left in London.

she recorded his impact on audiences. A typical entry reads: 'I never heard more genuine shouts and screams of laughter!'

Music hall performers came from, and performed, all over Britain. But it was to London that they headed if they sought to enter the stratosphere of fame and wealth. And in the roster of stars, the great proportion – Sam Cowell, Marie Lloyd, Dan Leno, Little Tich, Albert Chevalier, Harry Champion, Charles Coburn – hailed from the London area.

These stars could rely on a vast base of loyal London fans to support and boost their careers. Their comic acts drew on the humour of the London streets, the language with which their audiences engaged in their daily lives amplified back to them from the stage. And not just on the stage. Marie Lloyd, quintessential cockney gal, was celebrated for her off-the-cuff quips, which drew particularly on the East End tradition of cheerful insult. For instance, there was the occasion when Marie led a strike by music hall artistes. Another singer, Belle Elmore, flagrantly crossed the picket line outside the Coliseum Theatre. 'Let 'er in,' Marie shouted to the other pickets. 'She'll empty the theatre.'

Dan Leno Gardens, a park in Kennington, named after the outstanding male star of music hall. Several theatres were enlarged simply to provide extra room for the vast and guaranteed audiences who turned out to enjoy Dan Leno's comedy acts. The great crowd-pleaser's frequent command appearances in front of Edward VII earned him the nickname 'the king's jester'. When Dan died in 1904, the actor-manager Sir Seymour Hicks wrote: 'the world is poorer by a thousand laughs'.

The great Dan Leno poses outside his home, 56 Akerman Road, Camberwell, with two supporting players from the varied menagerie he kept at the address. He is dressed as one of his famous comic characters, The Railway Guard, an official who constantly harangued passengers while doing no work whatsoever. One of a series of collectible cards, from around the year 1900, packed along with packets of pipe tobacco.

By way of making audiences feel even more at home, the songwriters infused their titles and lyrics with the names of familiar London streets and landmarks. Some of the most enduring of music hall numbers – 'Knocked Them in the Old Kent Road', 'Down at the Old Bull and Bush', 'Let's All Go Down the Strand ('Ave a Banana)', 'Burlington Bertie from Bow', 'I Live in Trafalgar Square' – sound like sat nav directions around the capital.

Performers also drew on the varied personalities they observed while out and about in London. Dan Leno had a portfolio of songs based on the comic vagaries and absurdities of characters such as the Ice Cream Man, the Floor Walker, the Railway Station Platform Superintendent, the Racegoer and the Beefeater.

In these songs, the old city forms a backdrop to comical situations, exactly as it had in so many Elizabethan stage comedies 250 years earlier. For instance, one of music hall's biggest comic hits was a song inspired by London's relentless expansion in size and population. 'If It Wasn't for the 'Ouses in Between' was launched in 1894 by Gus Elen, who modelled his act on Sam Weller. An instant hit, it was taken up by many other singers. The performer boasts about his little garden, which would be the picture of rural solitude if it wasn't hemmed in by millions of other houses. Still, as the refrain assures us, the view is magnificent.

Oh it really is a werry pretty garden
And Chingford to the eastward could be seen
With a ladder and some glasses
You could see to Hackney Marshes
If it wasn't for the 'ouses in between.

The names of other London landmarks pop up like chorus girls as the proud homeowner turns to all points of the compass to take in the view.

> And 'endon to the westward could be seen
> And by clinging to the chimbley
> You could see across to Wembley
> If it wasn't for the 'ouses in between.

The Grand, Clapham. Opened in 1900, it is the last surviving purpose-built music hall in south London. Many music hall artistes chose to live in the Clapham area since the district gave easy access to theatres right across the capital. The Grand was built and managed by a consortium of local residents, including music hall comics Dan Leno and Harry Randall.

The association between music hall stars and London landmarks continued right up to the end. When Marie Lloyd died in 1922, her death coinciding with the rapid demise of music hall itself, many obituaries led with the same quote. It had been overheard by the critic James Agate, in an exchange between two commuters on a morning train. 'Marie. She had a heart as big as Waterloo Station.'

Presiding over London's comic life were two booming figureheads, one an unruly leader of misrule, the other doing his best to maintain order over that misrule.

Since his London debut around 1660 (see p. 27), Mr Punch, his wife Judy, dog Toby and sausages had comprehensively infiltrated the city. He had lent his name and image on paper, as the title and guiding spirit of the world's most celebrated humorous magazine. In puppet form, he was similarly inescapable.

Punch and Judy performances weren't confined to special events like parties and fairs. They popped up in parks, in public squares, along strolling places such as the newly constructed Embankment. Passers-by could watch, casually, for a few minutes, then go on their way, hopefully after tossing a penny into a bucket. A typical such scene, notable only for the identity of the passer-by in question, was observed by the showman and historian Alfred T. Story and recalled in a *Strand Magazine* article:

> Who has not spent a pleasant half hour watching the antics of Punch ... I once remember the Prime Minister [William Gladstone] lingering on the edge of a crowd in Parliament Street while the immortal drama was being enacted under 'the pale glimpses of the Moon'. It was a night on which there was an important debate in which the Grand Old Man delivered a telling speech and who knows but he made his points better for the two minutes he allowed his mind to relax by watching the exploits of the grand old hero of the kerbstone play that has run a greater number of nights than even Hamlet.

Music hall chairmen were taller than Mr Punch and almost as successful in grabbing the public's attention. The primary purpose of the halls was to serve alcohol. The primary purpose of music hall chairmen was to suppress any sign of alcohol-fuelled trouble. Bars ran the length of the building on either side of the audience area, allowing punters to move easily from one to the other. Unsurprisingly, trouble flared up easily.

The chief requirement of a chairman was a stentorian voice. The most successful chairmen could all silence a brawl with a single boom from the lower depths of their lungs.

The boom was followed by a second discharge, this time humorous. Chairmen took different approaches. John Read, resident chairman at Collins Music Hall in Islington, used song. At the first sign of trouble, he would burst into a suggestive ditty that was both off-colour and off-key. His great rival, Tom Tinsley of Gatti's music hall, claimed that brawlers would promise to stop fighting if he would stop singing.

For Harry Fox, chairman at the Mogul Saloon, alliteration was the key to controlling a rowdy Saturday night crowd. The music hall journal *The Era* compared Fox to a juggler. 'All else is forgotten as audiences hold their breath in disbelief at his verbal command and the endless stream of alliterative arabesques. How long can he keep his Os and his Ps and his Ms in the air, before a rogue letter brings the whole verbal cavalcade hurtling to the floor? Yet the breath cannot be held within forever, and ere long it erupts from the onlooker's lungs in an explosion of laughter worthy of a broadside from one of Her Majesty's battleships.'

Most of Harry Fox's introductions were spontaneous, or apparently spontaneous. But his opening speech, as he launched the evening's proceedings, was the same each and every night, always greeted with cheers and laughter, however many times members of the audience might have heard it previously.

'Welcome,' he would announce, 'to this mighty magnificent majestic musical mecca, the Mogul of Middlesex, to this monumental circus maximus of London merriment, the magnetic munificent midpoint of this metropolis of mirth.' His introduction became so widely quoted that the theatre changed its name to the Middlesex (then a widely used synonym for London). To continue the alliteration, the haunt of humour had become a monument to the 'metropolis of mirth'.

Metropolis of mirth. The term, in so many ways, summed up London throughout the nineteenth century. With striking symbolism, the publication of *The Pickwick Papers* coincided almost exactly with Queen Victoria's accession to the throne and, in due course, one of the great misquotes of regal history.

The statement 'We are not amused', so often attributed to Victoria, has no basis in fact. Indeed, the young queen had a capital sense of humour and fun. She, the era to which she gave her name and the metropolis of mirth over which she presided were most definitely, and massively, amused.

The Middlesex Music Hall, Drury Lane, in 1958 after rebranding as the Winter Garden. The theatre was the domain of the legendary chairman (master of ceremonies) Harry Fox. A reviewer wrote of Fox's act: 'the breath cannot be held within forever, and ere long it erupts from the onlooker's lungs in an explosion of laughter worthy of a broadside from one of Her Majesty's battleships'. The Gillian Lynne Theatre now occupies the site. (Gerry Atkins Collection)

The model for 'The Laurels' in Pemberton Gardens, Holloway. It is still recognisable as the subject of Weedon Grossmith's famous illustration in the humorous classic *The Diary of a Nobody*. The property is typical of hundreds of thousands of houses thrown up in London's fast-expanding suburbs throughout the latter part of the nineteenth century. The Laurels and its like catered for the equally fast-expanding army of bowler-hatted City commuters.

The original drawing of Mr Pooter's home, The Laurels, by Weedon Grossmith.

Above left: London's most recognisable landmark, the Westminster (now Elizabeth) Clock Tower was completed in 1859. The chimes of Big Ben were still a relative novelty when Gilbert and Sullivan's comic operetta *Iolanthe* premiered in 1882. For the first time on record, the clock tower took to the stage as scenery.

Above right: Wapping Old Stairs, a nearly perfectly preserved spot of Tudor Thameside on the north bank. Although unfunny in itself, the location inspired a popular comic opera, *Wapping Old Stairs*, produced at the Vaudeville Theatre in 1894.

Left: A scene from *Wapping Old Stairs*. Docklands lass Molly, in love with sailor Tom, is initially ignored by him. She follows Tom to sea, dressed as a male sailor, but gives herself away when she starts washing his trousers for him. (Love, naturally, triumphs in the end.) The show was based on a serious melodrama, but a reviewer wrote that 'the librettist, while softening its harsher scenes, has introduced in abundance the element of mirth'.

7

From Slapstick to Mass Media: Grimaldi to the BBC

As pictures first started to move, the cinema and comedy formed a symbiosis. They came of age together. Thanks to the First World War, London lost out to Hollywood as the capital of moviemaking. But the city could at least claim to have fathered slapstick comedy: the genre that turned Hollywood from a bunch of orange groves into a dictionary word.

The grave of Joe Grimaldi (died 1837), founding father of clowning, slapstick and traditional Christmas pantomime as still performed today. It lies in Joseph Grimaldi Park, alongside the Pentonville Road. Every great clown of the big top, throughout the nineteenth and twentieth centuries, acknowledged Grimaldi as the guv'nor. They continue to bear the nickname 'Joey' with pride.

Joe Grimaldi (see Chapter 5) occupies a niche in history as the genius who developed slapstick routines from chaotic knockabout, little short of brawls, into something infinitely more inventive. Among other comic effects, he devised no less than thirty-two different types of pratfalls, all of which became tools of the trade for subsequent comics. In due course they were adopted wholesale by Charlie Chaplin and the other silent-screen comedians.

Grimaldi also evolved that now-standard mainstay of stage and film farce, the climactic chase scene. Chases had been a feature of the Italian harlequinades but were balletic rather than comic. Grimaldi gleefully reinvented them for his own devices. Chase scenes, London style, involved the entire supporting cast in a carefully timed and structured routine, designed entirely to raise laughs. One observer recalled them as 'an organised mob – greengrocers, fishwomen, bakers, police – running in Indian style across the stage'. One other element should not be forgotten, since it was to prove crucial in the early twentieth century when London comedy conquered the world. Apart from the clicking of the slapstick (used to add emphasis to comic moments) and the musical accompaniment, Grimaldi's comedy was played silent. There was no dialogue. Indeed, the very absence of speech was a core essence of the comedy.

Initially, the absence of spoken dialogue wasn't a matter of choice. In the 1840s, as purpose-built music halls sprang up across London, the licensing authorities had moved in and imposed a ban on dialogue routines. They had been heavily lobbied by bigwigs of the older, 'legitimate' theatre, who didn't want the music hall impresarios to steal their trade or their actors (music hall impresarios paid better for talent). So, music hall entertainers were legally allowed to sing to their heart's content from the stage, but the law forbade

First put on display to the public in 1802 as a travelling exhibition, Madame Tussaud's waxworks rapidly developed into London's second most popular attraction after the Tower of London. From the outset, it was treated as a godsend by humorists. The cartoon *I Dreamt I Slept at Madame Tussaud's* by George Cruikshank envisages a wild waxworks-only party taking place in the small hours while London sleeps.

Madame Tussaud's moved into its current Marylebone Road location in 1884, by which time it had evolved into a national institution. It also continued to generate a regular flow of humour, as in this postcard from 1920. The two boys' game of one-upmanship takes its cue from Tussaud's best-known attraction, the Chamber of Horrors. A trip to Tussaud's used to begin with a joke. A waxwork doorman at the entrance fooled countless visitors who approached him for advice.

them talking. The chairman of the night, and he alone, was allowed to introduce the various routines and address the audience directly. This rule was enforced ferociously. In a disastrous moment of forgetfulness, the leading clown Delpini uttered just two words on stage, 'roast beef'. For this error, he was imprisoned.

It sounds draconian, but it was welcomed, tacitly, by most of the performers. Jugglers might be good at juggling, and comedians might be good at pratfalls, but they didn't necessarily have the lung power or the articulation of speech to boom to the top gallery of a cavernous auditorium as straight actors, drilled in Shakespearean delivery, were trained to do. Thus, it was that performers of every hue learnt to speak in every possible manner, except by word of mouth.

Grimaldi eventually retired, his body shattered and exhausted by all those pratfalls. His was the ultimate hard act to follow, and the Grimaldi style of comic extravaganza rapidly became extinct. But by then, the comic techniques that he had pioneered were an established staple of nineteenth-century pantomime. And then in the dying days of that century, another brilliant improviser arrived on the London scene, a man who projected the art of silent comedy into a whole new dimension, and into undreamed-of spheres.

That man was the impresario Fred Karno. Born Fred Westcott in 1865, he trained as a plumber before throwing over his apprenticeship to join a team of comedy acrobats. But it soon became apparent that his natural talent lay in production rather than performance. Ever the opportunist and ad hoc dealmaker, he transformed himself into an agent, then an impresario, and then...

'The power of comedy over all other types of performance, became crystal clear to me,' recalled the man who was to become the ultimate tycoon of comedy. 'So I thought to myself, why not cut out the clever stuff and stick to the pratting about.' From then on, Fred Karno put slapstick acts front and centre stage, and gave them top billing on his posters. At the same time, he made another, enduring, contribution, by creating a new form – the silent comedy sketch. 'Audiences love comedy, but they also love stories,' said Karno. So, he combined the two.

The first of Karno's extended sketches was called *Mumming Birds*. Launched at the Canterbury Music Hall in 1903, it was set ... in a music hall. A succession of character acts, each more dreadful and disorganised than the previous act, unrolls, to mounting chaos. Eventually, the stage is invaded by the tormented audience, who simply cannot endure any more.

The term 'comedy sketch' was devised by impresario Fred Karno to describe a new type of entertainment. It was first used with reference to *Mumming Birds*, initially trialled across London music halls in 1903. While short in terms of running time, *Mumming Birds* enjoyed a theatrical run that most full-length productions could only envy. It was still being performed in London in 1944.

Comedy sketch followed comedy sketch, with titles such as *The Football Match* and *The Guardsmen*. Karno quickly formed a band of gifted comedy performers to bring his sketches to life. As 'Fred Karno's Army', the gang became a byword for comedy. Among the members were the young Charlie Chaplin (who would later develop some of the Karno sketches as films) and an all-round performer from Lancashire, Stan Jefferson, later known to the world as Stan Laurel, of Laurel and Hardy. Stan would later comment: 'Fred Karno didn't teach Charlie and me all we know about comedy. He just taught us most of it.'

The centre of the Karno organisation was a cluster of buildings in Vaughan Road, Camberwell. The Fun Factory wasn't quite as much fun as it was intended to sound. It was in reality a place of hard graft and meticulous control. The mere reality, though, was remarkable enough. The Fun Factory operated as the corporate headquarters of a comedy empire which, at its zenith, employed 130 professional and well-paid comedians. Its assets included one of London's first fleet of branded motorbuses, used to whisk Karno's performers from venue to venue. The Fun Factory's workshops provided scenery and props for many other producers around the UK. Increasingly elaborate, these items often performed as comedy acts in their own right.

The Fun Factory also acted as a training academy for the next generation of comics. Ambitious young men, and not a few young women, found their way to the Fun Factory's gates, knowing that they really were passing through the gateway to fame and fortune.

Fred Karno's 'Fun Factory'. The site, in Southwell Road, Camberwell, is hardly changed since it was purpose-built in 1906 as the nerve centre for the Karno masterplan to unleash merriment across Britain. The custard-pie-throwing gag is said to have been devised within these walls.

Enthroned at his base in the Fun Factory, Karno was lord of an empire devoted to comedy and nothing but comedy. The one-time circus acrobat steadily turned from a mere mortal into a nationally recognised adjective. Karnoesque, or 'pure Fred Karno', became a byword for the comic undertow of existence, for those moments when ordinary living turns into farce. And not just life, but also death on the grand scale. A few years later, Fred's name would be invoked by ordinary soldiers on the Western Front, as they mocked, in song, the mass-murderous inefficiency of the high command:

We are Fred Karno's army
The ragtime infantry.
We cannot fight, we cannot shoot,
What bleedin' use are we?

In 1910, Karno, entrepreneurial as ever, took a bold step. He sent *Mumming Birds*, with its London cast, for an eight-week engagement at the Hammerstein Theatre in New York. English comedy had a dire history of failure on Broadway, but *Mumming Birds*, renamed *A Night in an English Music Hall* for its transatlantic engagement and headed by Stan Jefferson, was a sell-out success. (Produced under licence, Karno's sketches would eventually draw large audiences as far afield as Russia, Brazil and Argentina.)

The Royal Courts of Justice, the setting for Karno v. Pathé (1909), believed to be the first ever court case to involve artistic rights in the cinema industry. Pathé had filmed Karno's sketch *Mumming Birds* without consent or payment, as they openly acknowledged in court. But the company relied, instead, on a legal technicality to win its case. Since Karno's sketches were silent and, to a great extent, improvised, they had no written script that could be plagiarised. Karno lost on this basis, but Parliament immediately changed copyright law to cover the loophole.

A Night in an English Music Hall continued to run in one New York theatre or another for eight years. Karno's immediate response was to send a second shipload of his players across the ocean, this time for a booking at Broadway's Colonial Theatre. The new production, with Charlie Chaplin in its cast line-up, was named *The Wow-Wows*.

In one way, the American venture was to rebound on Karno. Both his leading comedy stars, Chaplin and Jefferson, quit the Fun Factory and stayed in America to contribute to a different type of fun. They had accurately judged the future of comedy.

Among those who came to see the Karno shows in New York were two budding film magnates with monosyllabic first names, one called Mack and the other, Hal. Both were natural entrepreneurs, cut in the Karno mould, and they were on the lookout for a product to sell. They weren't acquainted at the time, but the two men shared a common vision, as well as big ambition.

Both these young men were impressed by the potential of the new cinema medium. At the time, moving pictures, while still admired as a technological wonder, were underexploited as a form of entertainment. But Mack Sennett and Hal Roach both believed that, given the right material, film could conquer the world. And sitting separately in the Hammerstein and Colonial theatres, both men knew that they had found what they were looking for. Slapstick comedy sketches, Karno-style, could provide the perfect material for silent cinema.

By 1917, Chaplin confidently told the world, via a syndicated press release, 'slapstick ... through motion picture developments, has taken the lead in the world's entertainments'. And Chaplin, Sennett and Roach all readily acknowledged their debt to Fred Karno. He was, said Roach, 'the man who originated slapstick comedy. We in Hollywood owe much to him.' Hollywood would go onto bigger and grander things, but it was two-reeler comedies that first signalled the full potential of cinema. London slapstick theatre can claim to be the cradle of cinema for the masses – whether or not it got an onscreen credit.

One person who did not benefit was Karno himself. Charlie Chaplin and Stan Laurel settled in America, but Karno preferred to stay in London. His comic inventiveness had breathed new life into the world of music hall at a time when it was beginning to look tired. But as the two-reel comedies of Sennett and Roach unrolled across screens, audiences deserted live theatre en masse and headed for the cinema. When the talkies arrived in London in 1927, Karno was still resting on his laurels, endlessly restaging his silent farces (his son, Fred Jnr, kept them going as late as 1948). The once forward-looking impresario quickly started to look like yesterday's man, stuck in an old-fashioned world that was shrivelling fast. Hubris also helped to accelerate his downfall. He acquired an island in the Thames, Tagg's Island, and built a giant 'palace of entertainment'. Still firm in the belief that his very name would draw audiences, he dubbed this folly the Karsino. Karno evicted a number of gypsies who had camped out on the island. It was said that they had placed a curse on the place. If so, they were more successful than Karno himself. In 1925, Fred Karno went bankrupt. Ruined in London, the provincial boy made good and returned to his roots. He ended his days running an off-licence in Dorset.

The drink shop is rumoured to have been bought and presented to Karno by a man who owed his old boss a great deal, and knew it. This was the comic genius destined to be 'the most popular figure in the world', in the words of a 1921 article in *The Stage* magazine. The piece continued: 'Never since the world began has the name of one mere man been a household word in every ... corner of the world'.

The statue of Charlie Chaplin in Leicester Square. His character the 'Little Tramp' remains one of the most universally popular and widely recognised comic icons of all time.

Charlie Chaplin's rise from a childhood of 'extreme poverty' in the south London slums (coincidentally, less than a mile from the site of Karno's Fun Factory) is one of the great rags-to-riches stories of history. Charlie left the mean streets of Lambeth behind, physically, when he relocated to Hollywood. Yet in another, all-important way, he carried his childhood haunts with him, and they never left him. His comedy was drawn from and inspired by those London streets.

These slums of Chaplin's formative years hadn't changed much since they were portrayed, and denounced by Dickens. To live there was to be one of 'the people of the abyss', in Jack London's words. When Charlie was four, his father, Charles Snr, deserted the family, leaving his wife, Hannah, and sons, Sid and Charlie, in penury. The father was a moderately successful music-hall performer whose double life matched those of many others in the halls: jaunty entertainer on stage, violent alcoholic when away from the public eye.

Hannah had enjoyed a brief career on the music-hall stage herself, but she now had to eke out a new living as a seamstress. The poverty-stricken family found lodgings in Methley Street, Kennington, between an abattoir and a pickle factory. It was a shabby, noisome spot, but it would also prove an inspirational one. Two decades later, the image of this back street would be as familiar around the world as that of Buckingham Palace.

A lobby card (foyer advert) promoting Charlie Chaplin's 1917 short masterpiece, *Easy Street*. The set, featured in other Chaplin shorts, is a precise replica of Methley Street, the poverty-row London address where Chaplin lived as a child, and where life was anything but easy.

Charlie's talent and driving ambition saved him from growing up into a real-life version of the Little Tramp. He made his first stage appearance at the age of five. By his early teens, he was being hired regularly as a boy actor. He joined the Fred Karno company at the age of seventeen, and in no time at all was the company's top-billed player. On a second trip to America, and keen to add filmmaking to his skill set, he willingly accepted Mack Sennett's approach. Between 1914 and 1915, the wunderkind embarked on a ferocious round of two-reel comedy films.

The defining moment of Charlie's career came just a few days after his induction into the Sennett studios, as he made preparations for his second film, *Kid Auto Races at Venice*. He had played many roles in his short life, but now he was in search of a distinctive image. Rooting around in the Karno wardrobe store, he picked out an ancient bowler hat, a pair of baggy trousers, an oversized pair of boots and a fake moustache, so far deemed too small for the cameras. Charlie dressed himself in this motley collection and at that moment, almost as if he had been waiting in the wings for centuries to claim his right to inherit the earth, the Little Tramp sprang into existence. 'By the time I walked on [to the studio floor],' Chaplin wrote, 'he was fully born.'

There may have been some genetic trait at work here. Charlie's grandmother had been a hawker of old clothes. But, consciously or unconsciously, Charlie was also giving three-dimensional form to a visual memory. Photographs of the south London streets taken in Charlie's childhood years are liberally scattered with men who look just like the Little Tramp, almost as if the camera lens was some sort of natural magnet for stunted fellows in baggy trousers and battered bowler hats.

The Little Tramp swept the world with a speed that Napoleon could not have envisaged in his most megalomaniacal dreams. Charlie had his head down, churning out films for Sennett, so that, at first, he barely noticed the impact. It wasn't until he started to take account of the Charlie Chaplin comic strips in the newspapers, and the Little Tramp dolls in the window of the luxury toy shop on Wiltshire Boulevard, that he came to realise the extent of his fame. He learned that one New York theatre, the Crystal Hall, in Union Square, had turned its entire programme over to Charlie Chaplin films. (It never screened anything else for the next nine years. A Chaplin film, *Crippled Trouble*, was showing when the cinema burnt down on 4 March 1923.)

The extent of Charlie Chaplin's appeal was universal and extended far beyond just the cinema screen. Other starring vehicles included a children's comic devoted to 'Chuckles with Charlie'.

More important, even more so than that famous costume, is the Grimaldi legacy, the pantomime wizardry that Charlie breathes into the Little Tramp. The resulting comedy made the whole world laugh as never before, and that comedy was transmitted straight from the London streets of Charlie's boyhood. We have Charlie's own testament to this connection.

In a 1916 magazine interview, he explained how the origin of the famous Chaplin walk, inspiration for numerous 'walkalike' competitions around the world, was lifted directly from the London streets. (Charlie himself once, anonymously, entered a contest to emulate his walk. He came third.) An old man, a rough sleeper named Rummy Binks, used to earn a few coppers by holding horses at a cab rank. His service allowed the drivers to pop inside for a quick one at the Queen's Head in Vauxhall Walk (now Black Prince Road). Charlie's uncle, Spencer, was landlord of the pub, which stood a short distance from the lodging in Methley Street where Chaplin and his mother lived. Chaplin recalled:

> When I saw Rummy shuffle his way across the pavement to hold a cabman's horse for a penny tip, I was fascinated. The walk was so funny to me that I imitated it. When I showed my mother how Rummy walked, she begged me to stop because it was cruel to imitate a misfortune like that. But she pleaded while she had her apron stuffed into her mouth. Then she went into the pantry and giggled for ten minutes. Day after day I cultivated that walk. It became an obsession. Whenever I pulled it, I was sure of a laugh.

Chaplin also recreated his London childhood in another way. It wasn't just the people but the places that he replicated in the Californian sunshine.

In 1919, Chaplin, now rich and craving independence, opened his own studio. On the backlot, he created a permanent set, which came to be used as the background for some of his greatest films, including *Easy Street* and *City Lights*. At its core was a street T-junction that bore no resemblance to any location in the surrounding Los Angeles area. It was a reproduction of Methley Street, the London thoroughfare where Chaplin had lived in poverty with his mother and half-brother Sid. There was no reason why Charlie should have entertained happy memories of this spot, but he ensured that the reproduction was correct in every detail, and, like the original, it wasn't a pretty sight. Yet transformed through the imagination of one of its former residents, the grim, anonymous London street became a familiar haunt worldwide, the 'Every Street' to the Little Tramp's 'Everyman'.

Broadcasting House, Portland Place, the home of the BBC, opened in 1932, by which time more than half of British households already owned a radio. It rapidly became the fount of British comedy and introduced a new term into the language – situation comedy (shortened to sitcom by 1943). The Beeb's legendary comedy programmes *It's That Man Again* and *Band Waggon* (*sic*) were regarded as important morale boosters throughout the Second World War.

Band Waggon proved to be the BBC's first great success in the field of radio comedy. Starring the comedian Arthur 'Big Hearted' Askey (left), with the posh Richard 'Stinker' Murdoch (right) as his straight man, the show began broadcasting in 1938 and continued into the early war years. The central comic wheeze of *Band Waggon* was that Arthur and Stinker lived in a flat at the top of Broadcasting House. They treated the roof as their personal backyard. Here, they hung out their washing and kept a goat named 'Lewis'. ('What about the smell?' 'Oh, Lewis will get used to it.') The good-humoured tone of the show, and its huge popularity, allowed Arthur and Stinker to take the mickey out of even the most sacred cows, let alone goats. In one scene, Lewis charges and butts the considerable backside of the BBC's overbearing director-general.

8

War

The First World War, 1914–18

Since its re-emergence from Roman rubble in the ninth century, London had enjoyed, in comparison to other major European cities, a calm and peaceful life.

All this changed in August 1914. Suddenly, London faced an existential threat as a result of the new age of flying machines. Peter Strasser, the architect of the Zeppelin air raids, mooted the total destruction of the city. He declared his intention to replicate the Great Fire of 1666, using incendiary bombs made in Germany and therefore highly reliable. 'Nowadays there is no such animal as a non-combatant. Modern warfare is total warfare,' he announced. London was on the front line for the first but not the last time.

The British authorities were well aware of German intentions and of the crucial need to boost morale. They had precious few weapons in their armoury. But one mode of

The statue of the Duke of Wellington at Hyde Park Corner, with the Wellington Arch, one of London's best-known landmarks, in the background. The present version replaced an earlier, and grotesque, equestrian statue that was mounted on top of the archway. The subject of a torrent of abuse from the press and public, statue No. 1 was eventually banished from London. A French general, defeated by Wellington at the Battle of Waterloo, commented: '*Nous sommes vengés* [we are avenged].'

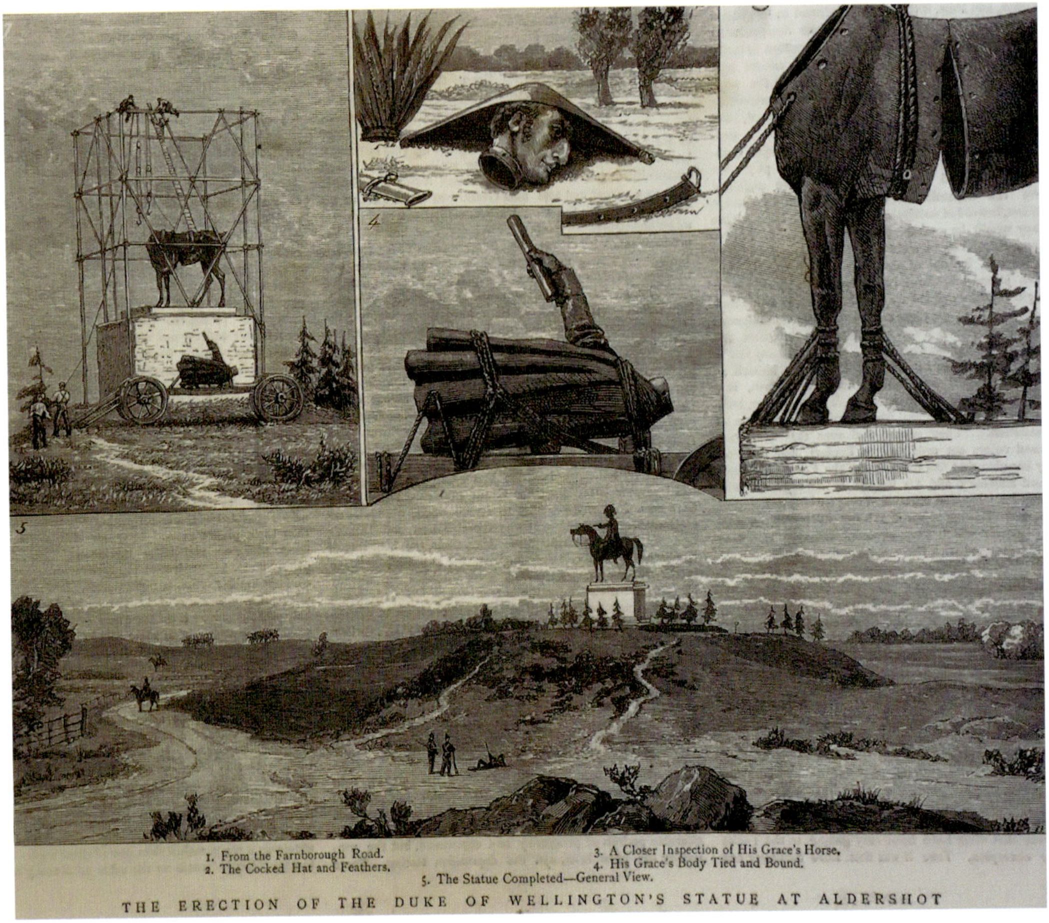

The statue of the Duke of Wellington, loathed and ousted by Londoners, is re-erected at Round Hill, Aldershot. Particular ridicule was attached to the duke's outstretched arm. Observing the dismantled stone limb laid out at its new site, *Punch* magazine compared Wellington's statue to Nelson's in Trafalgar Square. Noting that the naval hero had 'lost an arm to shot and shell', *Punch* observed: 'Now Wellesley's arm too, is, at Alder, shot.'

defence was fun and laughter. The authorities, dressed as if they were still in the frock coats of earnest and sober Victorian Britain, took a while to appreciate this, but cotton on they eventually did. The power of humour became inescapably clear in 1916 when the first collection of 'Old Bill' cartoons was published, selling a million copies in less than three months.

'Old Bill' was the quintessence of the veteran who had done time in the trenches. He was a curmudgeonly, walrus-moustached, mud-caked, balaclava-clad, pipe-smoking Tommy described by his creator as 'dull, dim and honest'. Above all, he was a survivor, a gruff old soldier who had somehow kept himself alive through years of the nearest thing to hell on earth yet devised by the human species. His gruff commentary on the war process endeared this little cartoon figure to front-line soldiers, who recognised themselves in 'Old Bill', and to civilians at home. He made millions laugh at a time when laughter was most needed. 'The Germans had a lot going for them,' an American diplomat is said to have remarked at the end of the war, 'but they didn't have an Old Bill.'

'Old Bill' was drawn from life. His creator, Captain Bruce Bairnsfather, was a graphic artist before the war and had served on the front line alongside the real-life Old Bills. He listened, watched and drew. The first batch of 'Old Bill' cartoons was dispatched to and published by *The Bystander*, a Fleet Street magazine. *The Bystander* promptly multiplied its circulation and developed a second revenue stream by selling prints of the cartoons. One cartoon in particular, 'A Better 'Ole', was set to become an icon of the war, second only in fame to the Kitchener 'Your Country Needs You' poster.

In August 1917, a play featuring 'Old Bill', which dramatised 300 of the best Bairnsfeather cartoon gags, opened at the Oxford Music Hall in Tottenham Court Road. Titled *The Better 'Ole*, it starred Arthur Bourchier, one of the leading actors of the day. The impresario C. B. Cochran recorded his first impression of the script. 'My wife asked me what was making me laugh so much. I read it to her. She laughed as I had done, and sometimes the laughter came through tears.' Audiences felt the same way.

London theatres had closed immediately on the announcement of war, but with the tentative support of the authorities, they swiftly reopened. The Christmas pantomime season went ahead unabated, only now the Prince Charmings all wore khaki and many of the panto villains bore surprising resemblances to the Kaiser.

Stage comics were among the first Londoners to sign up to the colours. Jack Melville had been a member of Fred Karno's troupe of comedy players before the war, but soon he found himself drilling in Hyde Park, along with hundreds of other raw recruits from every walk of life. He recalled the frantic chaos during those early days of the new, amateur army, notably the ill-fitting uniforms and the need to drill with brooms and spades in the

This unremarkable looking house in southeast London functioned as a powerhouse of humorous productivity across seven decades. No. 5 Bennett Park was both the home and the studio of the great comic artist Donald McGill, who churned out his famously rude postcards at the rate of ten a week, selling more than 200 million of them across his career. Despite his association with the saucier side of the seaside, McGill, born here in 1875, spent his entire life embedded in Blackheath and barely ventured to the coast.

Above: At the outbreak of hostilities in 1914, the prolific London artist Donald McGill, famous for his 'saucy' seaside postcards, diverted his talents to patriotic, morale-boosting cartoons. An artificial leg prevented McGill from serving in the forces. He made up for this with a cascade of knockabout postcards designed to keep Britain laughing. Images like this one, mocking the German Kaiser, proved a particular hit with soldiers at the front. McGill reworked the image during the Second World War, substituting Hitler for the Kaiser.

Left: London was on the front line throughout most of the First World War, and humour proved to be one of its key defensive weapons. This postcard was mailed in 1916, at the height of the Zeppelin air raids on the city and its outskirts.

absence of rifles. He couldn't help drawing parallels with the comic chaos of Fred Karno's stage sketches. Others saw things the same way. 'Fred Karno's Army' (see Chapter 6) was soon among the most popular of soldiers' songs.

Suddenly, comedy was a sellers' market. Old stagers, too venerable to join the forces, scrambled to answer the demand. The entertainer George Graves, who had previously specialised in light opera roles, was one of those who recognised the yearning for laughter. Early in the war, he remodelled his act into one of the first non-musical, standalone comedy routines. Viscount Sandhurst, the Lord Chamberlain (the official responsible for theatre censorship), went along to the Empire Theatre, Leicester Square, to observe Graves onstage. Sandhurst had been under pressure from a whole range of lobbyists to close down popular entertainments in the theatre as it was deemed to be detrimental to the war effort. But he was won over by Graves's effect on his audience, many of them servicemen home on leave. He even found himself laughing out loud. 'It is a bright show,' the Lord Chamberlain reported, 'and very much appreciated by the audience, among whom were very many soldiers and sailors ... Graves very clever and rather vulgar, but no harm'.

It was during this period that film comedies starring Charlie Chaplin gained a popularity previously unknown in the history of professional entertainment. His universal humour was grasped by millions as an antidote to the horrors and deprivations of the war. In military hospitals, special projectors were rigged up so that the films could be beamed onto the ceiling for the benefit of patients unable to sit up.

Londoners, like everyone else, loved Chaplin, but they also relished another great comedy star, one who, unlike Charlie, stayed in their midst throughout the conflict.

George Robey, master of a dazzling range of comedic roles, held sway as London's leading purveyor of laughter throughout the years of the First World War. Not for nothing was he billed as 'The Prime Minister of Mirth'.

Leicester Square, 1908. The domed building, top right, is the Alhambra Theatre, George Robey's domain. The site is now occupied by the Odeon Leicester Square, venue of choice for British film premieres. The porticoed building, top left, is the Empire Theatre, where the teenage Charlie Chaplin made his West End debut in 1903. The Empire's exterior – reproduced in Hollywood, California, for Chaplin's 1952 film *Limelight* – remains virtually unchanged.

George Robey was already an established star in 1914. A Londoner through and through, he had been born in Kennington Road, just a few hundred yards from the house where Charlie Chaplin was to enter the world twenty years later. George made his name as a music-hall comic. He became known throughout the land by his soubriquet, 'The Prime Minister of Mirth'. Then came the war.

Robey was forty-five, and too old for military service. This didn't stop him volunteering, to the great amusement of the recruitment sergeant, who recognised him immediately. 'I volunteered to prove my worth by running round the parade ground four times,' Robey told the press, patting his considerable pot belly as he made the statement. 'For some reason the sergeant laughed.' When the journalists had stopped roaring, Robey continued: 'Then I offered to lie about my age. For some reason, he laughed again. It was the one time in my career that I did not welcome loud uncontrollable laughter.'

Robey dominated London comedy throughout the war, both on stage and, egregiously, off. His comic stunts, always widely reported in the newspapers, made mirth out of the grim circumstances of wartime London.

Robey was hosting a fundraising rally in Trafalgar Square when a Zeppelin appeared in the distant sky and bombs started to fall. Robey looked towards the offending blimp and intoned: 'Shurrrrup. I'm trying to hear what I am saying.' Several witnesses swore blind that the Zeppelin promptly turned tail and fled back to Germany.

Robey despised warmongers. He had done voluntary work at Charing Cross station and seen the wounded men and the shattered corpses arrive by night. 'They are among the countless memories that make me want to kill a man who gasses in a general way about the splendid thing war is,' he recalled. He had a special contempt for the women who handed out white feathers to men not wearing military uniform. Robey bided his time. Then came the day when, walking down Regent Street, he was confronted by a woman clutching a bunch of white feathers. Pushing one of these into Robey's buttonhole, she demanded: 'Young man, you should be at the front.'

Robey promptly grabbed the woman by the shoulder and made a citizen's arrest. Summoning a passing policeman, he boomed in his most stentorian stage voice: 'Constable, years ago I made a promise to my dear mother to arrest any woman who accosted me in the West End. She is breaching the Streetwalking Act. Do your duty and lock her up.'

Robey's greatest contribution to First World War London was undoubtedly the succession of shows in which he starred. The hits started with *The Bing Boys Are Here*, continued through with *Zig Zag* and ended the war with *The Bing Boys on Broadway* (a London production, despite its name).

London's most popular show during the war was the lavish musical *Chu Chin Chow*. Audiences delighted in the romance, the lavish costumes and scenery. Robey's shows came a close second, but if it was laughter that was sought then there was no competition. The great comic also earned an honourable mention in that most celebrated of First World War fictions, *Journey's End*. A soldier announces his intention to catch *Zig Zag* as soon as he gets back to London. 'Harper saw it on leave. Says it's damned good. George Robey's pricelessly funny.'

The bells of London rang out on 11 November 1918 in celebration of the Armistice. A few days later, George Robey opened in a new comic revue, *Joy Bells*, launched in the same euphoric spirit.

Less than twenty-one years later, however, the bells once again fell silent.

The Second World War, 1939–45

Cue a scene from the 1941 film *Pimpernel Smith*. General von Graum, played by Francis Sullivan, is the official already appointed in advance by Hitler to be gauleiter of London following Germany's successful invasion of Britain. He is discovered for the first time in the film, at his desk, trying to get to grips with a key British defence mechanism. 'Know your enemy,' he intones. 'I am told that the English have a secret weapon. Their sense of humour. And I am determined to find out all about it.'

He then examines the work of P. G. Wodehouse, *Punch* magazine, Edward Lear and Lewis Carroll, concluding: 'When I am gauleiter of London, I will see to it that there is no talk of sense of humour.'

Buffoon though he is, von Graum has the right idea. Material like this proved to be not just funny, but morale boosting. It helped to keep London going, through the months when the city was once again on the front line, the very cauldron of hostilities. And Londoners were laughing, not just at the jests themselves, but at the very fact that they were laughing. After one of the worst nights of the Blitz, all the newspapers carried a photograph taken in

Punch.]

"*I reckon I'd sleep much better if I knew what time the first train comes through.*"

Punch magazine did its bit to keep the nation laughing through the hardships of the Second World War years. David Langdon's 1940 cartoon drew its humour from the thousands of Londoners who took refuge in Underground stations during the Blitz.

"*Aye—that's the famous Fifth Columnists' Gate.*"

Come peace, come war, the Tower of London continued to provide source material for humorists. A *Punch* magazine cartoon from August 1940, when invasion appeared imminent and Britain was on high alert for spies and saboteurs ('fifth columnists').

Throughout the Second World War, *London Evening News* artist 'Lee' (Joseph Lee) kept the city laughing with his daily cartoons. As with this example, printed at the height of the 1940 Blitz, Lee managed to extract mirth from even the most desperate moments of the war.

"Whose bright idea was it to leave Savage Central Africa this year?"

a severely damaged East End street (its identity censored). One shop bore the sign: 'OPEN AS USUAL'. Its next-door neighbour, a grocer, which had its windows blown out, bore an almost identical sign: 'MORE OPEN THAN USUAL'. Another much-circulated Blitz story emphasised the extremes of the London stiff upper lip. It concerned an elderly East End woman whose home received a direct hit from a bomb. Rescuers who dug her, alive, from the rubble discovered a full bottle of brandy, buried alongside her in the ruins. One of them pulled the cork from the bottle, ready to give her a medicinal sip. From her stretcher, the old lady bawled at him: 'Put it back. That's for emergencies only.'

Many decades later, at the age of ninety-five, the actor and radio host Nicholas Parsons was asked the secret of his longevity. 'People often ask how I survived so long,' he replied. 'Well, I was in the Blitz. Humour sustained me.' Yes, a sense of humour was indeed a key weapon in the city's armoury. Von Graum got just one thing wrong. There was nothing secret about it.

Throughout the war years, one figure reigned as the unchallenged king of London comedy. Tommy Trinder, a true warrior of humour, ruled the heart of London, both sentimentally and geographically, from his domain just off Oxford Circus.

TT's palace was the London Palladium. For over a decade, the Palladium had been billed as 'The Greatest Variety Theatre in the World', and even the kings of Broadway had

Comedian, actor and master of ceremonies Tommy Trinder reigned over the London Palladium from the mid-1930s onward. Unfazed by the onset of war, he continued to entertain audiences from the Palladium stage, even as bombs rained down on the West End. Trinder is pictured on the left of the front of the programme.

never challenged this title. Since 1930, it had been the venue for the Royal Command Performance, initiated in 1912. Trinder presided over the Palladium as if it was his personal property. (His personal stationery bore the address Tommy Trinder, c/o The London Palladium.) He doubled both as compère and live performer, a one-man double act that he returned to in 1955, when ITV launched *Sunday Night at the London Palladium*, one of the most popular shows in British TV history. His association with the Palladium lasted, on and off, for forty-nine years.

Trinder went out on a limb to assert his freedom to make jokes about the war. In 1943, he pulled out of one show, *Tommy Get Your Fun*, because censors demanded the cutting of one joke. He also ensured that Fleet Street laid hands on the joke, so that everyone got to hear it anyway. This was the offending item: 'I was walking down Whitehall the other day when an American soldier came up to me and asked, "What side is the War Office on?" I told him: "Our side, I hope."'

Far from being alienated, audiences at the London Palladium lapped up jests like these, not least because they knew that Trinder was sharing the perils with them. He remained up there on the Palladium stage, night after night, even when the bombs were falling on the West End. The Luftwaffe united him and his audience in a bond of mutual danger, as the laughter almost drowned out the sound of explosions. Thirty years later, when London was suffering a new wave of bombings, Trinder, now making jokes about the IRA Provisionals, remained as unabashed as ever.

Once again, as so often in the history of London humour, an iconic figure in comedy was drawing his material from the everyday life of Londoners. Londoners responded

The BBC's most popular programme throughout the Second World War was the comedy show *It's That Man Again*, known universally as *ITMA*. *ITMA* managed to capture the wartime atmosphere and distill it into much-needed laughter. Its anchorman, comedian Tommy Handley, became a household name, second only to Winston Churchill. While Tommy did his best to maintain some sort of order, a host of eccentric and unruly characters kept bursting into the script, spattering catchphrases everywhere. They included the boozy Colonel Chinstrap ('Don't mind if I do'), the charlady Mrs Mopp ('Can I do you now sir?') and the ever-miserable Mona Lott ('It's being so cheerful as keeps me going').

with gratitude, recognising him as one of their own. Trinder's credentials as a street-level Londoner were impeccable. The son of a Streatham tram driver, he left school early to work as an errand boy at Smithfield meat market. By the age of seventeen, he was touring the variety circuits as a fully professional comedian, and his showbiz career developed exponentially from then on. But he never lost the language or the outlook of an ordinary working-class Londoner, or the ability to connect with the huge working-class audiences who shared his background. Early in Trinder's career, the manager of Brighton Pier refused to take his act, dismissing him as 'just a common cockney'. Exactly.

But Trinder's appeal transcended class, and he was frequently invited to entertain the Royal Family at Balmoral and Windsor Castle. They adored him too, not least because he didn't crank down his cheeky chappie approach in their presence. Introduced to George VI, Trinder reminded the monarch of an earlier royal performance, when the king was still Duke of York and Trinder himself was up and coming. 'You've climbed very high since then,' the King said. Ever the dab hand at ad libs, Trinder replied: 'You haven't done so badly yourself, sir.'

Trinder was only thirty when the war broke out, but his ability to keep London laughing meant that he was considered too valuable an asset to conscript for the forces. He already embodied the humorous cockney in the same way that Sam Weller had done a century earlier. The prototype hadn't changed much since Dickens's day. The resourcefulness, the resilience, the warm heart and, above all, the instant wit – Trinder had all these in spades. Now these qualities gained an extra dimension when the lights went out and London became a wartime city. By the end of the war, Trinder had become the emblem of what the broadcaster Richard Dimbleby called 'the unvanquished cockney spirit'.

Trinder's popularity meant that he was quickly co-opted into the ranks of movie stars, and he spent the war years tirelessly shuttling between film studios during the day and the Palladium stage by night.

In 1943, he starred alongside James Mason in *The Bells Go Down*, a tribute to the London firefighters who had tackled the conflagrations of the Blitz and often sacrificed their lives in the process. Trinder played a not very successful bookie who finds a new grace and purpose in life when he signs up to join the fire brigade.

Much was made of the fact that Tommy's character actually dies at the end of the film. He is first up the ladder into a blazing warehouse, which then collapses on top of him.

The day before *The Bells Go Down* opened in the West End, Trinder plugged the film from the Palladium stage. 'I've never done a death before,' he told the audience. 'Rubbish,' shouted a heckler. 'You die every night, right here.'

On Victory in Europe night, Tommy Trinder was the natural choice when the BBC sought a radio commentator capable of summing up the spirit on the streets. All through that joyous night, he reported live from the streets on behalf of the BBC Home Service. When the conflict was at its height, Trinder had borrowed and reworked a phrase from Vera Lynn when he advised Londoners to 'keep laughing through'. They followed his advice, and demonstrated to the likes of General von Graum that humour was, indeed, a weapon, not just for survival but for victory.

The six members of the Crazy Gang, four of them born-and-bred Londoners, came together in 1932. An overnight success, they reigned for almost four decades as one of the most enduring British comedy acts. Their greatest single success came with the 1941 film *Gasbags*, made at Shepherd's Bush, in which the gang's fish and chip van becomes attached to a barrage balloon, inadvertently helping to win the war in the process. Bud Flanagan, one of the gang, enjoyed a late-life career bounce when he was invited to sing the theme song to the beloved BBC sitcom *Dad's Army*.

"'It's a topping morning, Jeeves.' 'Decidedly, sir.' 'Spring and all that.' 'Yes, sir.'"

Above: Jeeves and Wooster, the evergreen comic duo created by humorous novelist and short story writer P. G. Wodehouse. Their leisurely Mayfair world has all but vanished, but their comical adventures still attract readers around the world. Wealthy idler Bertie Wooster shares his Berkeley Street flat with valet Jeeves, whose vast store of wisdom, knowledge and diplomatic genius are constantly called upon to get affable boss Bertram out of his latest scrape.

Right: Buck's Club, Mayfair, the main inspiration for the fictional Drones Club, a key locale in P. G. Wodehouse's *Jeeves and Wooster* stories. The facade of the Drones may be dignified, but within lurks boisterous mayhem. A haunt for overgrown schoolboys with lavish inheritance trust incomes, the Drones is a minefield of practical jokes, while the dining room is subject to a constant hail of bread rolls. Bucks Fizz was invented at the club – the real-life club, not the Drones.

9

A Legacy of Laughter

Humour had sustained London through two wars and was considered so important to morale that it was treated as an instrument of policy. Now it was called upon again to help lift the mood of the city. If anything, the need was greater. The bombs and rockets had ceased, but in the years that followed 1945, life turned grey. Food rations were sparser and morale actually lower than during the war years. For the millions living in the dreary, battered city, comedy provided an alleviation. Certainly, the appetite for it remained as strong as ever. *The New Yorker* magazine correspondent Mollie Panter-Downes told her readers: 'The big funny-man shows starring the English comedians Tommy Trinder and Sid Fields are ... booked for weeks ahead'.

London Evening News cartoonist 'Lee' marked the end of the Second World War with this drawing in which Mr Average Londoner presents a heartfelt submission outside 10 Downing Street. Londoners had suffered endless privations throughout the war, not least the dreadful Woolton Pie which formed a staple part of their diet. They felt that they were entitled to their own 'London Civilian' contingent at the Victory Parade down Whitehall.

An even more crowd-pleasing show arrived in town in 1951. This was the Festival of Britain, designed to provide a 'Tonic to the Nation' after the deprivations of the war and post-war austerity. On the South Bank site rose the world's then largest free-standing dome, alongside the iconic 'Skylon', a 300-foot-high blade of steel that gave the impression of floating in mid-air. The tone of the festival was that of a passionate headteacher, exhorting their pupils to ever-higher exam results. Various exhibits stressed British contributions to science, technology, manufacturing, agriculture, the high arts and design.

Sensibly, the organisers also recognised and saluted humour as well. The exhibit that attracted the most visitors – almost more than all the others put together – was the Far Tottering and Oyster Creek Railway.

Almost 3 million festival visitors enjoyed a ride on this transport of delight, despite the fact that it looked as if it was about to fall apart at any moment. The miniature tribute to rural slow trains was a 3D, steam-emitting embodiment of the much-loved *Punch* cartoons by Rowland Emett.

Emett, a real-life version of Wallace in *Wallace & Gromit*, was a bit like a human incarnation of the Far Tottering railway. He was gentle and modest, but also an engineering genius who could make anything work. The little railway was a *pièce de résistance* of whimsical creativity, and it seemed to sum up Britons' view of themselves at that stage. Other nations, like the USA, would have packed their festival full of bombast. But Britons were happy to accept the FTOCR as a sort of emblem of the country – gently charming, a bit slow and sleepy in places, eccentric, certainly, a touch rickety, but getting by courtesy

The whimsical Far Tottering & Oyster Creek Railway proved to be the hit of the 1951 Festival of Britain.

The trackbed of the old Far Tottering & Oyster Creek Railway passes through a rewilded and unfrequented section of Battersea Park. Chelsea Bridge, teeming with traffic, lies just a few yards to the right.

of a range of second-hand items; dreamlined rather than streamlined. Its popularity with visitors spoke for itself. And in the end, the railway proved to be anything but tottering. It worked efficiently enough to carry almost 3 million visitors on time and without mishap. Via humour, Rowland Emett's model railway thus underlined another aspect of British self-identity: 'Don't underestimate us. After all, we won the war.'

Londoners also left their own humorous imprint on the festival, commenting that the 'floating' Skylon was like the British economy, 'with no visible means of support'.

While the crowds trooped around the festival's worthy displays about national chicken production and the like, a whole new formulation of British genius was being cooked up in a Westminster pub.

The Grafton Arms, Strutton Ground. In the early 1950s, the Westminster pub was a mecca for comedy performers, writers, and producers, including a quartet of pals consisting of Spike Milligan, Peter Sellers, Harry Secombe and Michael Bentine. The unique style of pub banter conjured up by this foursome developed into *The Goon Show.*

The Grafton Arms was managed by Jimmy Grafton, the latest in a line of pub landlord Graftons. The family had owned the business since 1848, and pulling pints was in the blood, but Jimmy also doubled as a part-time comedy scriptwriter. As a result, his pub regulars included a wide, loud, lively and hard-drinking collection of comedy professionals. Among these was a quartet of pals headed by Spike Milligan (who lived in a flat above the pub), along with Peter Sellers, Harry Secombe and Michael Bentine. Their freewheeling banter, punctured by voice impressions of all and sundry by Sellers, caught Grafton's ear. Under his guidance and influence, the wacky pub chatter of the Grafton Arms was picked up and beaten into shape to become a BBC radio series. *The Goon Show* (initially, and understatedly, titled *The Crazy People*) launched in May 1951, coinciding almost to the day with the opening of the Festival of Britain. A new chapter in the history of humour had been opened.

Surreal comedy, such as it was before the Goons, had always been a very British proposition. It had literary antecedents in the works of Laurence Sterne, Edward Lear, Lewis Carroll and the *Daily Express* columnist 'Beachcomber' (J. B. Morton). But it was the Goons who launched it into the age of mass media. The effect was profound and enduring, and felt as far afield as Hollywood. It proved a key influence on the Monty Python team, and it continues to inspire modern comedy writers. And, in due course, it was to change the very character of London itself.

Spike Milligan, known as 'the father of alternative comedy, was the driving force behind *The Goon Show*. His surreal vision permeated British comedy throughout the second half of the twentieth century and acted as a particular source of inspiration for the *Monty Python* team. Spike is memorialised in the gardens of Avenue House, Finchley, close to his home of many years. His bronze statue sits on a park bench, just as he was wont to do in real life, ready to chat to all comers.

For Milligan, the main Goons' scriptwriter and ideas man, the premise was simple enough. Surreal humour, with its crazy juxtapositions, manic dialogue and far-out plots, was just a reflection of real life. It proved 'by fabricated insanity that nothing could be as mad as what passes for ordinary living'.

The (real-life) first encounter between Milligan and Secombe rather illustrates his point. The pair had both served as Royal Artillery squaddies in the North African campaign. Milligan's unit accidentally allowed a large howitzer to roll off a cliff, landing near a radio truck in which Secombe was seated. 'Suddenly, there was a terrible noise as if some monstrous object fell from the sky quite close to us,' Secombe recalled. Then a flap opened in the side of the truck and Milligan's face appeared. 'Anyone seen a gun?' he enquired. Secombe's response: 'What colour is it?'

The Goon Show ran across seventeen series and gathered very substantial audiences between 1951 and 1960. Among their openly declared fans was Prince Charles. The future king even contributed a foreword to the book *Growing Up with the Goons*.

Balham, a typical and unremarkable London suburb, owes its fame to the qualities espoused by the Goons. In the famous spoof *Balham, Gateway to the South*, Peter Sellers mocked the style of gushing travel documentaries which trawled the globe in search of exotic locations. Balham was presented as a colourful cornucopia of tourist attractions, full of strange ancient rituals, such as toothbrush drilling. Balham's response takes the shape of 'Impressions of Balham', a series of plaques in Station Road. They too draw on the sheer ordinariness of the place, celebrating subjects such as shopping and going to bed, but without the sniggers.

The famous facade of Ealing Film Studios, tucked away in the leafy West London suburbs. 'The Ealing Comedies', made here, set out to capture on film the gently humorous tenor of life in the immediate post-war years. Their locations also moved away from the smart Mayfair backgrounds which had been the main backdrop for pre-war films set in London. Instead, they featured settings such as the bombed-out London docklands (*Hue and Cry*), Clapham lodging houses (*The Lavender Hill Mob*), Lambeth (*Passport to Pimlico*) and King's Cross St Pancras (*The Ladykillers*).

Above: The Whitehall Theatre in 1957. For almost two decades, the theatre was the hotspot house for stage comedy in London. The term 'Whitehall farce' became generic and was also adapted to describe the shenanigans in the Houses of Parliament just down the road.

Left: Possibly the most amusing grave site in London is the Highgate Cemetery burial place of Douglas Adams, author of *The Hitchhiker's Guide to the Galaxy*. While neighbouring graves bear floral tributes, Adams's is adorned with items that celebrate his droll approach to the cosmos. As those familiar with Adams's sci-fi comedy know, '42' is the answer to the meaning of life, and the mass disappearance of ballpoint pens poses one of the great unsolved mysteries of the universe.

A theatre close to the Palace of Greenwich commemorates two great twentieth-century Londoner comedians. Bob Hope, born in Eltham in 1903, went on to cross the pond and become, in the words of First Lady Nancy Reagan, 'America's most honoured citizen and our favourite clown'. The theatre was renamed in his honour in 1982, after direct fundraising by Hope saved it from closure. Frankie Howerd, born in York but raised in Eltham, made his debut on the theatre's stage at the age of seven. At the time, it was known more modestly as Eltham Parish Hall.

However, radio's grip on the entertainment market was in steep decline. TV was taking over as the main mass entertainment medium. For once, the Goons got serious. How could the show go visual?

The first stab at an answer was *The Running Jumping & Standing Still Film*, released in cinemas as a 'second feature'. Starring Milligan and Sellers, it provided a half-hour of visual comedy like nothing audiences had ever seen on screen before. But Goons fans felt instantly at home.

Among fans both of *The Goon Show* and *The Running Jumping & Standing Still Film* were a Liverpool foursome who, in a few years' time, were to find themselves among the most famous folk on earth. From the word go, the Beatles regarded themselves as something of a comedy, as well as music, act. John Lennon was to bring the house down at the 1963 Royal Command Variety Performance when he invited the audience at the London Palladium to participate in the group's final number, 'Twist and Shout'. 'The people in the cheaper seats, clap your hands. And the rest of you, if you'd just rattle your jewellery.'

On tour, while still a support act, the band even made their own short Goon-style films. It helped to fill in long waiting periods backstage and kept crews and fellow performers laughing. A typical example found the heroine, Georgina (George Harrison), tied to railway tracks by the dastardly Sir Jasper (John Lennon) and rescued by Fearless Signalman Paul (guess who). So, when it came to choosing a director for the first Beatles film, the boys immediately demanded Dick Lester. Nobody else would do.

A Hard Day's Night, and subsequent Dick Lester films, both captured and helped to spread the legend of 'Swinging London', of which Beatlemania was such a key part. In the early 1960s, all sorts of historic evolutions collided and fused to transform the character of the ancient city almost beyond recognition. Some of these influences, like hippiedom and the sexual revolution brought about by the pill, were international. Some, like Minis and miniskirts, homegrown, or to be exact, home reduced.

Shops and streets vibrated to the sound of the new working-class bands. Transistors and tannoys ensured that there was no escape from the sound. The most visible aspect was an explosion of colour in a metropolis that had once placed the notion of reserve on a pedestal. No one worried any more about looking respectable in grey suits or shunning vulgar pinks and saffrons. Much of the city gave the impression of an early rehearsal for *The Rocky Horror Show* or *Hair!* Even the graffiti turned to pop art styles. Londoners, dazzled by all this colour and unseated by the speed of change, began to behave in zany ways, much like characters from *The Goon Show*.

Goonish humour, born a decade earlier, added the final element to the mix. The legend of 'Swinging London' was perpetuated via cinema screens around the world, thanks to *A Hard Day's Night* and the later Beatles' film *Help!*, along with *The Knack*, *Smashing Time* and the Oscar-winning *Tom Jones*, which offered madcap 'Swinging London' eighteenth-century style.

Much of the humour of the 'Swinging London' films was based on genuinely surreal moments, spotted, in passing, by the director, the writer or the performer and fed into the scripts. A regrettable example, straight from life, occurs in *The Knack*. A line of monks, on a visit to the big city, are glimpsed queueing up at a contraceptive machine.

'Swinging London' was effervescent and also, inevitably, like all style-dominated eras, evanescent. In due course, it gave way to the punk era. Goodbye surreal humour, hello anger and cultivated aggro. Punk heroes like Sid Vicious weren't interested in laughs. But sixties' London, where everyday life could take on the nature of a non-stop silent film comedy, is caught forever in the comedies of the time, with their wild gags and updated versions of Chaplinesque slapstick.

The crazy sixties stand as the last period when it is possible to discern a uniquely London brand of humour. The great architectural symbol of the time was the 1965 Post Office Tower, essentially a giant telecommunications mast wrapped in a trendy piece of design. The tower lay at the heart of the global telecommunications age, then expanding at warp speed. The tower provided the setting for a key moment in the 'Swinging London' comedy *Smashing Time*. But it also signalled the end for London as a romp city. The Post Office Tower enabled and enshrined this new age of global media, into which London hurtled with relish. Any remaining sense of insularity vanished. Noel Coward's 'old, grey city' became a truly international metropolis. The city's humour went the same way. Its distinctive features blurred, faded, vanished.

Before this happened, however, there emerged one last comic creation, a humorous cartoon figure who embodied London life as millions of Londoners knew it.

Opened in 1964, the BT Tower (formerly Post Office Tower), looming above Fitzrovia's eighteenth-century terraces, immediately became a symbol of 1960s tech progress. It also became a key location for comedies of the time. These included *Kitten Kong*, the Goodies' spoof of monster movies, in which the tower is felled by an overgrown kitten.

The Bristow comic strips were a key feature of the *London Evening Standard* for thirty-nine years and were syndicated globally. The little bowler-hatted buying clerk was a Londoner, but he carried instant recognition factor for office workers the world over.

Bristow was – is, for though of his time, he remains immortal – a little bowler-hatted clerk who commutes every day to central London to work in the buying department of a large, impersonal office. Bristow is the ultimate anonymous nobody, a nonentity's nonentity. Herein lies the recognition factor that was to bestow celebrity status on this low achiever. It turned his cartoon strip into a worldwide franchise, but Bristow never lost his identity as a typical Londoner.

Appearing daily in the *London Evening Standard* from 1962 to 2001, Bristow became part of the warp and woof of London life. The little clerk's creator, cartoonist Frank Dickens, poured out strips by the thousand from his studio in the Barbican. Dickens's sister worked in various London offices, and every Monday they would meet up so that she could regale him with material for the next batch. The supply never threatened to run dry.

Millions of commuting office workers laughed at Bristow, knowing full well that by so doing they were laughing at themselves. The hierarchy of post-war London office blocks was merciless, the working environment drab. But Bristow doesn't see himself as either humble or crushed. He gets through the day thanks to jokes, daydreams, silly office pranks, inventive forms of idling and ridiculous ambitions that he can never hope to realise. His is the same uncrushable London spirit that another Dickens portrayed in the shape of Mr Micawber.

But Bristow's world, the nine-to-five London of conformity and rigid hierarchy, was fast receding into the past. Bowler hats were becoming an endangered species. Londoners continued to laugh, but perhaps no longer at London specifically. London humour in the twenty-first century is world humour. Its laughing stock is no longer itself, at least for now. But it has retained the centuries-old sense of itself as a not-too-serious city. That has given it a bedrock of humour, and, out of that, good humour that forms a permanent core of its identity.

London still laughs, but it laughs at the same things as New York or Rome. The distinctive London characters, the jolly cockneys and the cheeky clerks, have joined the array of other London ghosts. For now, at least, London's discrete own-brand humour has become a matter of history, another element in the rich loam of its heritage, rather than a live, developing force. But the power to raise a chuckle, a guffaw and even a belly laugh can still erupt in the here and now. For anyone who enjoys exploring history on the ground, London is still the 'metropolis of mirth'.

The photographs in this book are a reminder that in this city of stone and brick monuments, London's humour, too, has its fair share, although they tend to be rather more colourful than the average memorial.

One such is the auditorium of the Palladium theatre. This is the theatre, virtually unchanged, that was the concert hall of laughter during the Blitz, when London most needed laughter. In war and peace alike, it has reigned as the fulcrum of London humour. The Palladium has played host to laughter-makers from around the world, from the USA, France, Denmark and even, save the mark, Scotland. But in the final days of the Palladium as the palace of varieties, it was another breed of 'foreigners', the Merseysiders, who conquered the city. The Beatles took the lead. They were followed by their pal Ken Dodd, who descended from Merseyside to inherit Tommy Trinder's crown as the king of the Palladium, and thus, by extension, chief London laughter-maker. He swiftly became an institution of the London summer.

The London Palladium at Christmas, still very much in business after 115 years as a mecca for comedy. It was here that the world woke up not just to Beatles' music but Beatles' humour when the band burst onto the celebrity scene at the 1963 Royal Command Performance. From the stage of the London Palladium, John Lennon invited the audience to join along with 'Twist and Shout'.

It has been claimed that, here in the Palladium, 'Doddy' raised the longest sustained laugh ever heard from a London audience. Like most things to do with the evasive subject of humour, the claim is impossible to pin down. But whatever the truth of the matter, the joke is reprinted here, upside down, to allow readers to prepare for the effect.

Here's Adam and Eve. Cuddling up. All alone together in the Garden of Eden.
Eve purrs: 'Darling, you do love me, don't you?'
Adam thinks for a bit. Scratches his head.
'Well,' he says, eventually, 'There's no one else, is there?'

Little Ben, a miniature, Disneyfied version of the House of Commons clock tower, is strategically sited in front of Victoria station. Visitors arriving in London via the cross-Channel ferry are greeted by this quintessential piece of British whimsy. The mood is further enhanced by lines of verse inscribed on Little Ben's base.

International visitors to London are given a crash course in the British sense of humour, courtesy of these lines of light verse set into Little Ben. They take the form of a mock apology for British summer time, which has caused many a French person to miss their train: 'My hands you may retard or may advance/My heart beats time for England as for France.'